THE NORWEGIAN'S DIARY

The Norwegian's Diary

*How a Garage Sale Discovery Revived Lingering
Questions about America, Immigration, and Free Will*

DANIEL PAWLEY

RESOURCE *Publications* · Eugene, Oregon

THE NORWEGIAN'S DIARY
How a Garage Sale Discovery Revived Lingering Questions about America, Immigration, and Free Will

Copyright © 2024 Daniel Pawley. All rights reserved. Except for brief quotations in critical publications or reviews, no part of this book may be reproduced in any manner without prior written permission from the publisher. Write: Permissions, Wipf and Stock Publishers, 199 W. 8th Ave., Suite 3, Eugene, OR 97401.

Resource Publications
An Imprint of Wipf and Stock Publishers
199 W. 8th Ave., Suite 3
Eugene, OR 97401

www.wipfandstock.com

PAPERBACK ISBN: 979-8-3852-2630-6
HARDCOVER ISBN: 979-8-3852-2631-3
EBOOK ISBN: 979-8-3852-2632-0
VERSION NUMBER 10/14/24

Every effort has been made to contact copyright holders. However, the publishers will be glad to rectify in future editions any inadvertent omissions brought to their attention.

This book is dedicated to my immigrant grandfathers, Arthur G. Bauslaugh and Victor M. Pawlowski, both whom as men of faith, courage, and integrity survived and thrived amid spiritual challenges and brutal work conditions of 19th and 20th Century America.

"I think I made a mental commentary on the American civilization at the close of the 19th century, but hardly think it was commendatory thereto."

—Ollis Evenson, July 4, 1897

Contents

Prologue | 1

CHAPTER ONE
The Incident at Raymond and University Avenues | 7

CHAPTER TWO
An Awakened Pause in Springtime | 13

CHAPTER THREE
The Mood of Destiny | 23

CHAPTER FOUR
American Immigrant Ecclesia | 33

CHAPTER FIVE
Mercy Please | 42

CHAPTER 6
EXTRA! Join or Die | 53

CHAPTER SEVEN
Contexts of Survival | 64

CHAPTER EIGHT
Clinging to the Myth of a Departed Captain | 73

CHAPTER NINE
Labor and Lament | 84

CHAPTER TEN
Disquietude into Silence | 95

Epilogue: Fragments of a Finder's Diary | 107

From the Author | 123

Selected Bibliography | 125

Index | 133

Prologue

DEAR CHRISTOPHER,
Can you believe it? Twenty-five years have passed since you wrote to me expressing your shock at seeing the words of your ancestor, Ollis Evenson, featured in a 1997 issue of *Books & Culture ~ A Christian Review*. I remember being thrilled myself that my old article, "The Diary of an Immigrant," had reached out to readers who had interests in American immigration stories. But none compared to hearing from an actual Evenson descendant who had familial knowledge of Ollis, his journey to America in the 1800s, and his life of faith and hope mingled with sadness and regret.

It's a story that has stayed with me, possibly because I am now, all these years later, an *emigrant* myself, from not to America, and I have often wondered if Ollis had been happy with his decision to leave Norway. Did he wish ultimately to return there as a *remigrant*? Did he wish he had never left? Did he wonder if he had chosen the right destination, the United States, and at the right moment in history, the late 1800s? Would he have wanted to go somewhere else if given the opportunity? Did he end up feeling it had been the biggest regret of his long life? Answers to those questions are elusive, of course, though the questions themselves are relevant to all who choose an immigration path they feel they must take, at any age and for any number of reasons. I would like to explore some of them in the pages ahead.

But I'm getting ahead of myself.

The Norwegian's Diary

Books & Culture, an insightful review of Christian thought which gallantly tried to expand its truncated subculture, went out of business a few years ago after a two-decades run. And since it was published in discardable newsprint, you may not have saved the article in preservable form. So, to refresh your memory, allow me to recount how it came to be.

On a placid summer morning at the picturesque canoeing pond of Como Lake in Saint Paul, Minnesota, I had stopped to visit an estate sale held in a green-shuttered, courtly-white house overlooking the lake. This was a regular weekend activity for me, and my goal was always to find good books I could acquire cheaply. I once found a first edition of Nathaniel Hawthorne's *Mosses from an Old Manse* and in fact negotiated the price down to almost nothing. That was a rare find, however, and most of the time my browsing simply led me to titles that nurtured my cross-discipline curiosity to know something about topics of which I had little or no knowledge.

The community surrounding Como Lake was a proverbial gold mine for books. Located midway along the tree-shaded, north-south avenue connecting Saint Paul's numerous liberal arts colleges, and nearby Luther Seminary, those mature neighborhoods housed generations of hungry minds and books left behind by dearly departed souls. But you had to get there early before the used-bookshop owners from Saint Paul, Minneapolis, and the river town of Stillwater swooped in to gather up the best of them.

Long story short, I had on this particular morning spotted a cardboard box containing a cache of works by Mark Twain, seemingly overpriced, and subsequently lost my negotiating battle to a buyer who said he would pay the full amount. As he moved Twain to his canvas collection bags, however, I noticed something else on the floor of the box: the diary. Your ancestor's diary. Ollis Evenson's diary. I paid pocket change for it and, forgetting about Twain, began to read. How often do you find something amazing like this? I thought while wandering through the old house. Then, back home, I read the complete diary before the weekend was out and,

PROLOGUE

in the days ahead, caringly crafted the article about it for *Books & Culture*. That's the story.

Diaries.

Do you keep one, Christopher? I do sporadically, but mainly to remember travel experiences that I fear will be lost among the photographs I take (check out the Epilogue of this book). Rarely do I record the day-to-day of ordinary life.

But I love to read all diaries. Here in Portugal I have a bookshelf full of personal ones that eventually found their way into publication through the efforts of the diarists' family members, friends, interested historians, and other third-party sources who determined there was human value in releasing the primary document to the public. Some, similar to Ollis's, were left by Scandinavian-American immigrants like Iduna Bertel Field, whose *Recovered: A Century-Old Diary*, scribbled in a 19th century Minnesota farm house, also included thirty raw poems articulating the adventures and pains of immigrant life inclusive of a mental health subtext. Another, *The Diary of Elizabeth Koren, 1853–1855*, published a century later in 1955 and reprinted seven times, was fairly brutal from the moment she stepped onto the ship in Norway until trying, often unsuccessfully, to find a peaceful life in rural Iowa. Still others, such as Roger Andersen's *The Immigrant's Journey*, possess a fictional aspect built on an ancestor's diary entries to draw out the drama of what it was like to cross a precarious ocean, arriving in an unfamiliar land of both promise and terror that tested one's survival skills at the height of the Industrial Revolution. Interesting, all, and the best ones are diaries that were never intended to be published and have never been edited, redacted, or otherwise filtered by external framing.

I think of these as *message-in-a-bottle* diaries.

Ollis's personal diary is an example. It, as I'm sure you must know, had been a re-print project by another Evenson family member who had rescued the fragile, handwritten pages of the original diary, typed them up inclusive of Ollis's misspellings and incorrect grammar, and sandwiched the manuscript between bright red covers held together by plastic comb binding. That was

The Norwegian's Diary

the diary I found. The uncorrected spellings and grammar from Ollis's broken English gave it an authentic, unfiltered aspect, and I would not have been put off in the least if the word *GENUINE* had been stamped on the front cover. (I'd hate to think how my own immigrant diary would read if I tried to write it in Portuguese.)

I'll add that most of the personal diaries on my shelf were edited for publication, thereby compromising their authenticity. They're still interesting, but here's the thing: a personal diary, like a personal prayer, needs to rest on nothing other than the sincerity of personal intent. It can't be critiqued or altered by anything external to the veritable, bona fide truth emanating from the diarist's soul. So, in most cases, it's going to be rough, imperfect, all over the place in its execution, but ultimately and beautifully true. It can't, moreover, have been a rehearsal for publication, seemingly like Henri Nouwen's, *The Genesee Diary* (as engaging as it may be), or all done up like *Divine Mercy in My Soul* by Maria Faustina Kowalska, *The Flame of Love* by Elizabeth Kindelmann, or even *The Secret Holocaust Diaries* by Nonna Bannister (as lovely as they all are).

It has to be, I'll repeat, an authentic message in a bottle, as it were, untouched by anything other than the individual who wrote it, metaphorically rolled it up, sealed it in an unsinkable bottle, and set it free on the ocean of time and existence. Wherever it drifts is where it will be found, and whomever finds it will be the undesignated recipient of its message, whether it is one of hope, sadness, despair, survival, or merely the story of a self-examined life that says, for what it's worth this is what I was about. Only then can it be written about by its finder, in this case, me.

So, Christopher, here, a Portuguese immigrant from America in the year of our Lord, 2023, I have set my mind to reexploring your ancestor's amazing diary one more time to know and contemplate its messages, as though I were the one who had reclaimed it from a stormy sea and now am witness to its truth.

I'll close by mentioning that I had immigrant grandfathers, one who traveled to America from the Poland-Ukrainian borderland, the other from Scotland via Canada, though to my

PROLOGUE

knowledge they never kept diaries. I wish they had because they had much to say about America in earlier times. They loved their adopted country, I think, but there were moments when that love found itself tested and occasionally sacrificed on the often harsh and sometimes cruel altar of real life, in their own *promised* land, no less.

As ordinary men in their day, they worked menial jobs in impossible conditions, wrested a survival living from that daily torture, raised families amid tragedy and turmoil, and tried to self-educate themselves through disciplined study when time and circumstances allowed. They were also men of faith, and had they kept diaries they, like Ollis's, would assuredly have articulated a prayerful recognition of joy and thankfulness but also lived adversity and diminished certainty.

In fact, *prayers in a bottle* might be the most accurate description that comes to mind for understanding the essence of a diary well kept.

I can live with that.

Yours sincerely,
Daniel

Lingering Question 1: Can a lone personal diary illuminate history?

Short Answer: Collectively, *immigrant* diaries, for instance, form a basis for understanding history, as some of the greatest historical literature rests on diaries and their companion sources: personal letters gathered in the research process. The lone diary, however, has to possess remarkable clarity of insight and vision to be considered essential. The best ones, though, offer something wondrous: unedited thought. Many years ago, the famous economist, Peter Drucker, offered a statement that has stuck, now paraphrased. If you really want to know the soul of history, he suggested, sit down and read the work of mediocre novelists who expressed their time and place, unpolished. His examples were Anthony Trollope and Theodore Dreiser. Drucker may have been referring to an unvarnished quality evident in writing that could have been improved

5

aesthetically through editing and revision, but that historical lucidity and emotion would have been lost in the process. The personal diary, like the personal letter, moreover, might be seen to offer something similar: rare truth that speaks precisely because it emerged privately and honestly and was never tinkered with by its source. Sometimes truth is *true* because it is left alone, untouched. As such, it shows itself over time to be historically valid and essential.

CHAPTER ONE

The Incident at Raymond and University Avenues

ON THE EVENING OF November 21, 1919, Ollis Evenson, six months and one day shy of his seventieth birthday, was struck by an automobile and—by his own account—nearly killed. He had been riding his bicycle across the busy intersection of Raymond and University Avenues in Saint Paul, Minnesota, when the vehicle interrupted his nightly ride from work to home. Later, he wondered how close to death he had actually come, though "thank God," he wrote in his diary, "I only lost about two square inches of skin on the back of my right hand. The driver did not even look back, but sped on like a streak of blue lightning."

It was the second time in just a few years that this American immigrant from Norway had been almost flattened by the chaotic city traffic common in early 20th century America. And though Ollis never provided a verbal sketch of that chaos, we can easily picture it from having seen footage depicting the mayhem of congested civic corridors. Black-and-white newsreels, now posted ubiquitously online, show the daily peril of pedestrians trying to navigate a passage to *safety islands* in the middle of busy thoroughfares. Model T Fords, penny-farthing bicycles, old Lippert-Stewart delivery vehicles, and electrified streetcars loading and dropping off passengers, competed with each other in as many as eight unmarked lanes of traffic choked with exhaust and engulfed in deafening clatter.

The ease of being knocked down and out by traffic was part of the American free-for-all mentality during those years, a time when the country proved that it was never quite ready for its inventions and innovations. Technology moved faster than social awareness and the simple protection of people, as it does even today. If Bill Loomis of *The Detroit News* had been present in 1919 to console Ollis, he would likely have reminded him that "there were no stop signs, warning signs, traffic lights, traffic cops, driver's education, lane lines, street lighting, brake lights, driver's licenses, or posted speed limits" at that moment. Road speed was not yet understood, left turns were a haphazard experiment, and driving while drunk was neither prosecuted nor condemned. In the absence of such dangers, Ollis, like thousands of others, learned about them the hard way: by being struck down. Perhaps committing the incident to his diary was his way of consoling himself.

The incident was also by no means the only personal knockdown he wrote about in his approximately fifteen hundred diary entries spread between 1897 and 1923, minus a few missing years.

The onslaughts of physical pain, emotional loss, family tragedy, and perhaps most troubling of all for him personally, the spiritual frustration of an American immigrant longing to nurture his best parts—his spiritual parts—seemed to wear away at his soul like breakers eroding a seashore. The diary entry from the 4th of July 1897, which serves as the epigraph to this book, alluded to that side of the story: "I think I made a mental commentary on the American civilization at the close of the 19th century, but hardly think it was commendatory thereto." This was a "mental commentary" borne from frustrated attempts to self-educate and to build a healthy inner life against all the external forces America had to offer: the physical demands of daily labor, the mental chaos of rapid technological change, the psychological noise of an expanding media culture, and the emotional turmoil of domestic life and trying to raise a family.

THE INCIDENT AT RAYMOND AND UNIVERSITY AVENUES

Spiritual frustration, one could say, was bound to dominate the end of a century that had begun in Jeffersonian optimism and ended in post-Civil-War realism. It was also bound to continue into the early decades of the following century, which were the primary years of Ollis Evenson's diary.

Indeed, the harsh, working-class life within America's twin mind traps of capitalism and industrialization was, alone, enough to have immigrants packing their bags for a return to their home countries as remigrants. The "relentless, shoving, pushing, threatening" labor culture, not to mention "supervisors who used fines or dismissal as weapons" and the overall "unsafe working conditions" of the era, had transformed the desire for economic betterment in America into the craving for some sense of spiritual return to lands left behind, according to *Round-Trip America: The Immigrants Return to Europe, 1880–1930*, by Mark Wyman. "'America has robbed me of my glory,'" quotes Wyman, citing the story "The Imported Bridegroom" by the Lithuanian Jewish writer Abraham Cahan, about a remigrant who was part of the spiritual frustration of Jews who felt there were too many roadblocks to the meaningful practice of their faith in America. Complaints by other remigrants mentioned by Wyman spoke about a lack of churches and quality time for religious observance, the absence of religious instruction in schools, and a secular climate ruling out "the ideals of religion," all contributing factors to social ills such as emerging racism and hateful newspaper content. "Truth and justice are very little respected in America," according to a Swedish immigrant of conscience who grew appalled by "lying newspapers and unpunished crimes as well as attacks on 'negroes.'"

Ollis, of course, was neither Swedish nor Jewish; nor did he give any verbal indication that he wished to return to Norway as a frustrated remigrant. However, themes within Wyman's book, and others such as Susan J. Matt's *Homesickness: An American History*, echo throughout the diary, and other immigrants who also kept diaries and wrote letters seemed to speak for all immigrants who craved a life of faith and spirit beyond the one-dimensional economic betterment offered by America.

The Norwegian's Diary

Matt quotes a female immigrant from Poland who urged her father to abandon his dream of an American life. "Oh, how lonely I am!" she wrote. "Here you only hear the noise of thousands of people walking, of the whistling of factories, of the bells of trolleys, of the whistling of traders in place of nightingales and larks. Instead of roses, tulips and lilacs [you find] barrels of garbage and covered wagons, and stench instead of fresh air." And when another immigrant from Sweden wrote home, she said that she "had to be careful about getting tears on the paper." Statistics acquired by Matt had revealed that as many as 50 percent of immigrants, from places as diverse as Japan and southern Europe, wished to return home during the years of Ollis's diary. Even pre-Holocaust Jewish immigrants, who had never been fully integrated into countries within eastern Europe, saw benefits in returning to places less alien than the United States during the late 19th and early 20th centuries.

Matt points out that simple nostalgia, familiar cultural products such as unavailable foods, the memory of festive events, and family members left behind, all fed homesickness among immigrants at that time. Unwillingness to adapt to conditions in America, moreover, drove others to commit their minds only toward returning home. They belonged in their countries of birth, many concluded, going back to familiarity with life lessons learned from the civic and rural cruelties imposed on them by a survival-of-the-fittest mentality. This was a frame of mind that was easy to criticize by immigrants who chose to gut it out in the factories and on the streets, though even the most hard-boiled survivors had to admit that America had become more like an impersonal agency than a spiritually fulfilling fellowship.

"I have not yet been happy in America! I am always sad and lonely and I look forward to the day and the hour when God will assist me . . .," wrote an immigrant from Poland, according to Matt. But where was God in America? That, for many, was the question. If traces of the Almighty could not be found in workplaces, markets, rustic rurality, or chaotic avenues swelling with crowds and noise, the resulting spiritual crave would need to be satisfied, where else, in faith communities. This was the real motivational context

The Incident at Raymond and University Avenues

of the explosive growth in America's ecclesial environment during the Industrial Revolution which had attracted so many throngs of immigrants to its shores. If you came, stayed, and struggled, you had a good chance of finding your way into a church or synagogue somewhere as a matter of survival. And you had many emerging choices.

Loneliness, homesickness, guilt, melancholy, and a pressing need to connect both to a severed past life and an uncertain future were all part of "a theologizing experience" brought about by immigration, as implied by Timothy L. Smith, a historian quoted by Matt. Old world traditions such as religious festivals, the celebration of patron saints, and the recasting of childhood rituals into new contexts, did more than facilitate meaningful nostalgia, too. They relieved the pain and healed the bruised, beaten soul. A Jewish immigrant brought forward by Matt echoed the essential truth of the wounded, a truth existing beneath ritual: "I went not in order to pray to God but to heal and refresh my aching soul.... Sitting in the synagogue among *landsleit* and listening to the good cantor, I forgot my unhappy weekday life, the dirty shop, my boss, the bloodsucker, and my pale, sick wife and my children. All of my America with its hurry-up life was forgotten."

Ollis Evenson would likely have identified strongly with this comment. Replacing the Yiddish landsleit of Jewish worshippers with the Norwegian fellowship he had found among Christ-following immigrants, his story reflected the same "aching soul" hoping to be healed by God. The hope was there. The life in America was a challenge, but challenges could be accepted, met with courage and resilience, and overcome. The opportunities residing within the proverbial American Dream might also be realized.

Of course, years later, being almost seventy and lying scraped and bloodied at the intersection of Raymond and University Avenues on that evening in 1919, he would likely have had other thoughts swirling in his mind, too. Who was he, really? Was he simply the 19th century Norwegian immigrant of his diary, who felt he had owed it to himself to risk what so many others had risked: the exchange of familiarity and low-growth stability for a fresh start in an unknown land of seemingly unlimited opportunities? Was he that lingering Viking soul he wrote about periodically over the years, following an ancestral urge to fulfill his destiny by traveling great distances on the open seas in search of unknown rewards? Was his ethnic backstory even more ancient, harkening back to the chaotic worlds, destinies, fates, rebirths and resurrections in so many of the Norse legends with which he was likely familiar?

Here he was, in any case, aware certainly that he was nearing his life's end, which painfully included one more knockdown in the American city he knew best, and where most of his existential drama played itself out before all of his human drama had ceased.

Lingering Question 2: What was, is, and likely will continue to be America's single most prominent message to itself and to the world?

Short Answer: Many would say, freedom. Many would say, opportunity. Many would say that America is still the one place in the world where, under the right conditions and with a forward-looking mentality, most people can arrive on its shores or landmass with nothing and gradually work their way to the top of some chosen profession, accompanied by all the psychological and material rewards such an ascendancy can provide. As idealistic as this sounds, it is still mostly true. However, success inevitably calls for measurement, and in America the most prominent measure will always be financial gain: money. The prime measure is not education, altruism, artistic and spiritual fulfillment, the appreciation of time, or even the reverence for life itself. It is money, or more specifically *moneyism* (the use of money as the rubric for evaluating standards of meaning), apart from which all other rewards so greatly pale in comparison that they end up bruised and bloodied, run over by the prime mover of self-realization in America: the almighty dollar.

CHAPTER TWO

An Awakened Pause in Springtime

THE SPRING SEASON IN Saint Paul, at least in Ollis Evenson's time, made its arrival during the latter part of May. That can still happen today, but in Minnesota where temperatures have increased 0.2 F° each decade since 1895, spring tends to show up in April or even late March. Winters can still be long and cold, and springs early or late, though year-round residents of the state say it's not like it used to be even thirty and forty years ago when one could count on a long winter followed by a definitive spring.

Early or late, springtime in Saint Paul features a colorful cornucopia of flowering crab trees, greenery that evolves from early fern to mature forest, silvery lake ice melting into wetland teal, and crocuses, geraniums, marigolds, and cornflowers to complete the botanical tapestry. Whether or not this tapestry existed as vibrantly in Ollis's day is not known, but the springtime mood of being suddenly awake from winter slumber, and well before the aliveness of summer and the reflective nature of fall, was something undoubtedly shared by all residents of the city.

So, it was not surprising in this awakened state that he grew reflective. It was his birthday, and he was thinking about Norway:

The Norwegian's Diary

> May 20, 1897: Today is my Birthday, being 47 years old. I may say right here, that I was born on May 20, 1850 on a farm named Froag in Nordorhov, Norway, about 30 miles northwest of Christiania, the Capital of Norway. The house in which I was born was taken down some 8 years afterwards and rebuilt a short distance away on the island in Lake Juvern, where I have reason to believe it still stands.

Committed to the diary just weeks before his July 4th entry and its unkind assessment of American life, the nostalgia of this entry undoubtedly provided reflective comfort for Ollis. A few sentences later, he mentioned his arrival in Saint Paul on August 16, 1880 with his brother Charles, who continued farther west to settle in Tacoma, Washington.

We never learn why the brothers diverged geographically, or why they left Norway in the first place, and so we're left with many questions. Were they fleeing European social upheavals of the 19th century, which in Norway had produced social and political challenges such as the Thrane Movement, a revolutionary labor rebellion led by the Norwegian journalist and author, Marcus Thrane? Were they wishing to get away from the regionally notorious Lutheran domination of church and faith? Was Norway's economic stagnation, and its limiting of vision and success especially among young people, the motivator? Or, was it the promise of "rivers flowing with milk and honey," "trees that grew silver dollars," or any number of mythical assurances which had infused the emigrant drive to America during the 1800s? For Ollis and Charles, we simply do not know.

We do know, however, that Norwegians had traveled to America, first in small numbers but later in multitudes, during the hundred-year period commencing in the 1820s, subsiding in the 1920s.

Driven in part by a shortage of arable land in the mother country, large-scale Norwegian emigration to the United States began in the 1860s, peaking two decades later in the 1880s and again between the years 1901 and 1910. So, Ollis and Charles

An Awakened Pause in Springtime

joined the throng in that second major migration. Proportionally, Norway's rate of emigration during those high-volume years exceeded that of every European country with the exception of Ireland and Italy. Irish emigrants to America had numbered over four million, from 1820 to 1930, while Italians came in just under that figure. By 1920, Norwegians departing their less-populated land of seafarers and farmers, fjords and fertile valleys, amounted to over seven hundred thousand, a staggering figure for a country barely exceeding two million by that time.

Odd S. Lovoll's *The Promise of America: A History of the Norwegian-American People* tells this grand-scale story as the son of a Norwegian halibut fisherman, an emigrant to Seattle, and an editor at the Norwegian-American Historical Association.

His volume, as visual as it is verbal, features a Norwegian-American church picnic on the front cover, an image of smiling children proudly waving flags of Norway on the rear. In between are Norwegians gathered on loading docks, in riverboats, on ocean sloops; walking next to transport wagons, building wood-frame houses, harvesting farm products in rural communities; worshiping in churches and reading dictionary-thick books through wire-rimmed spectacles on winter nights. Maps, newspaper clippings, and enticing advertisements ("10 Recruits Wanted . . . Town of Primrose . . . $170 CASH IN EXTRA BOUNTY") complete the pictorial narrative before we even settle into the verbal text of Lovoll's history. Settle in we do, however, as internal chapters enrich our appreciation for the Norwegian-American story. "Cultural Growth," "The Press and Public Life," and especially, "The Spirit and the Mind," are notable.

While the famed literacy rate among Norwegian-Americans may have been exaggerated, as Lovoll admits in "Cultural Growth," learning how to read and write well was always emphasized. An immigrant might even aspire to the writing of books, but such pursuits would likely have to co-exist with menial jobs that kept bread on the proverbial table. That was certainly the case for Ollis, who lived to study, though his life-of-the-mind cravings were ever squelched by long, frustrating hours of workforce labor. Physical fatigue and mental suffocation were his daily enemies. He often tried to rise above them, according to the diary, though with only limited success.

Lovoll also explores the Norwegian-American infatuation with newspaper reading and publishing. Here, we're talking literally about hundreds of broadsheets and tabloids with names such as *Scandia*, *NYE Norge*, *Sioux Falls Posteu*, *Western Viking*, and *Tacoma Tidende*, distributed through newsstands and by subscription. Some of the papers evolved into larger, durable enterprises. Some ceased publication. But in the spirit of popular, common-citizen discourse, all newspapers "created contact and promoted solidarity within the immigrant community, and they educated immigrants to become politically conscious," according to Lovoll. Political movements such as temperance societies and prohibition grew from the spirit of reform energized in part by newspaper culture, enlisted in turn by politicians who took what information they could to drive their campaigns of growth and change in America.

Ollis himself was a prodigious newspaper reader, though there are no indications in the diary that they were the main feeder of his politics. In fact, he seldom spoke of politics, other than to condemn slavery and lynching in the American south, and to speak of his corresponding love for Abraham Lincoln. Whatever political views he may have held, moreover, came from the well-expressed spiritual hunger he satisfied through book-reading and church involvement. He read scholarly sources on history and theology, participated in church even on snowy, sub-zero Sunday mornings, and enjoyed being a lay preacher when his minister was absent. As the receiver of Ollis's *message in a bottle* diary, I identify strongly with these activities as both of my immigrant grandfathers were readers and took turns in various capacities of lay church leadership. My Polish-Ukrainian grandfather, Victor, lent his thick east European accent to his church in Hamtramck, Michigan, while my Scottish-Canadian granddad, Graham, lay-preached regularly in the Detroit city rescue missions.

An Awakened Pause in Springtime

Congregational life for Norwegian-Americans "was central to their existence in America," says Lovoll in "The Spirit and the Mind." Participatory opportunities abounded, nurturing language development, practical and theoretical education, and social engagement for immigrants. Ministers became community leaders, respected for charting a course from the experiences of internal fellowship to the disciplines of external learning which expressed themselves through the founding of schools, academies, colleges, and universities. A clear trajectory from faith to knowledge had been established, and as with Ollis in his diary, this was the essence of a spiritual commitment one wanted most in his or her life, even if nurturing it ran up against the impediments imposed by work and existential obstacles.

Herein was exactly the crushing reality for so many immigrants.

They wanted more.

But they got less.

And it was too late to start over.

All forms of emigration, immigration, and remigration ask the same key question: Is the journey more about where you're going to, or more about where you're coming from? More simply, is the journey more about seeking, or more about escaping?

Living among American emigrants to Portugal and Spain, I ask this question almost daily. In real-time conversations, and in comments gleaned from internet boards such as *Americans in Portugal ~ The Expat Group* and *Americans in Spain*, the debate seems fairly balanced; though currently in the 2020s the escape side expresses its expat rationale more forcefully. Escapees cite perceived American ills such as "a neo-fascist takeover," "guns, public shootings, and availability of assault rifles," "political violence," "toxic people," "idiocracy," "racism," "poison food," "expensive medical care," "anti-science," "conspiracy theories," and "the January 6, 2021 political insurrection." An August 2022 study published in *The Portugal News* adds, "Most of the respondents we talked to expressed their growing unease with the social and political upheaval in the US. They are losing hope in the current political system, and they don't anticipate any significant change very soon." Charles Taylor Harris, author of the study, also cited cost-of-living issues such as not having access to affordable food in the US, healthcare costs, and insurance rates.

The seeking side, on the other hand, seems less energized by current events driving the need to escape, but more durable in its expression of vision for the future and the desire for enduring life satisfaction. "Reclaiming lost heart and soul," "growing personally from real-world education," "gaining a better grasp of history," "stepping away from one's comfort zone," "enjoying a new sense of community," "living in a café culture," "eating simple, healthy, affordable food," "resting in peacefulness of daily life," and "feeling close to many cultures and countries," are cited by members of the online communities mentioned. According to Harris, 90 percent of all respondents said "getting residence in Europe" was the paramount desire, and 47 percent "stated that quality of life is the main reason that helped them identify their destination."

A small faction in Harris's study, 10 percent, would consider renouncing their US citizenship, and consistent with my own observations of online expats, this desire for permanent closure is real. On August 1, 2022, Jillian M. wrote on *Americans in Spain*, "I am going to renounce my US citizenship and hope group members can give me any tips about what is required at the Embassy." Craig R. answered, "Good for you. It will be costly but I understand your decision. I too have thought about it."

Bringing this discussion back to Ollis, of whom we know little about his original motives for emigrating to America, we have to guess as to what they were.

Seemingly, we can eliminate *the escapee rationale* for him. Not even once does he say something negative about his country of birth. He does, however, wax nostalgic on occasion, using phrases like "my dear old mother Norway," and at one point says he'll be "a proud descendant of the Vikings" until his dying day. He also appeared to celebrate stereoscopic technology which allowed him to view Norwegian landscape scenes in 3D, transporting him back to the land he left behind. Incorrectly, he referred to the images

An Awakened Pause in Springtime

as "stenoptican," perhaps conflating the word "stenoptical" with "stereoscopic," the 19th century technology which combined two images to produce a 3D effect when viewed through a stereoscope. Despite these instances of nostalgia, though, there are no indications in the diary that he ever made a serious attempt to return to Norway even for a visit. But in that regard, we have to acknowledge the cost-prohibitive expense of such ventures for common people up to at least the 1920s, and Ollis mentions several times that he was "a poor man."

Thus, *the seeker rationale* fits him better.

Being thirty years old in his year of emigration, 1880, the prospect of shipping out to a new land of opportunity and reward must have engaged his imagination as it did with so many European emigrants.

The context for this forward-looking vision included opportunities for self-assertiveness, independence, personal advancement, and many other positive abstractions easily visualized through the widespread distribution of advertisements and printed images. Concrete opportunities, such as *The Homestead Act* of 1862, raised the stakes to an even higher, non-abstract level whereby emigrants could envision the promise of land ownership in America merely by living on and improving up to 160 acres of government-surveyed real estate. Those who researched this opportunity knew that speculators and railroads, logging and mining companies, got most of the land, yet small, ordinary farmers could also take part in the dream by committing to five years of residence on available soil.

Ollis, of course, was not in possession of a homesteader's land vision, according to the diary, as his goals seemed simpler, more urban, and more employment-related. However, the quality of an immigrant's personal vision did not have to rest on the acquisition of land or any other measure of economic prosperity. Religious freedom, forward thinking, and inspired vision for human progression were equally valid measures.

Here, it is worth fast-forwarding a hundred years to acknowledge a contemporary person's experiences as a Nordic immigrant in America, noting certainly that while life changes immensely during that time, basic ethnicity of mind and temperament, less so. Anu Partanen's journalistic memoir, *The Nordic Theory of Everything ~ In Search of a Better Life*, correspondingly offers a vivid image of Scandinavians who are much-attracted by American ambition and energy but ultimately disappointed by the country's lack of a more humane social contract between its haves and have nots. Nordic peoples have always "yearned to be free" in places of "energy and creativity," she writes. They crave that "fair shot at success" and the experience of "satisfaction in one's own achievements," so viable in the global image of life in the United States. And the intellectual and political heroes from history, inclusive of the moral rightness within the American founding fathers' democratic vision, is viewed as "a beckoning" to people who still take seriously the mantra of "government of the people, by the people, and for the people."

All of this "fills you with a can-do spirit," "irrepressible optimism," and "an abundance of positive thinking," Partanen adds, speaking for masses of dour, sour Nordics. On the eve of her emigration, she contemplated the journey ahead: "I would get to experience the most powerful country in the world firsthand, and start a new chapter of life, away from the safety and complacency of Nordic ways. I would be one of the huddled masses yearning to breathe free, one more participant in the greatest experiment on earth: building a truly diverse nation in which people from all over the world live and work side by side, united by their love of liberty and the chance to excel."

Where the dream began to erode for Partanen, once she settled into her new life, occurred when she came face-to-face with unanticipated American anxiety. People working long, irregular hours; widespread "gaps" between the treatment of women and men in the workforce; financial insecurity among almost everyone; the prolonged burden of paying off educational debts; severe problems of affording to raise children in America; and constant confusion from trying to balance the potential rewards of living in the United States with the psychological reality of personal "angst"—all left her in a permanent state of dizzying imbalance. Toward the end of her story, she weighs *the good* and *the bad* as if by stacking reasons on both sides of a balance scale, asking the question, "Does it really have to be a choice between these two?" She closes by stating that she "might want to stay forever" if America adopted simple Nordic ideas which produce "a healthy society."

Similarities of mind and outlook abound between Anu Partenen's personal reflections and Ollis Evenson's diary thoughts of a century-plus earlier, with the exception of one huge underlying factor: religion. Faith produced by the internal spirituality of a Nordic immigrant plays no role in *The Nordic Theory of Everything*, whereas for Ollis it was an inseparable factor of his most important cognitive experiences. In feeling and fervor, he seemed very much a descendant of the ancient Norsemen who worshipped Odin, their supreme god and "the consciousness of northern folk" as described in *Tales of Norse Mythology* by Helen A. Guerber. To an even greater degree, he seemed anchored in his lingering past as a Viking who had joined his compatriots in their well-studied conversion to Christianity. However, unlike Vikings who converted for opportunities of European trade and because of political pressure, Ollis's faith in a living Christ defined the totality of his life. His faith renewed his soul on a daily basis, and we continue through the diary with the timeless thoughts of Hebrews 11:1 (KJV) in mind: "Now faith is the substance of things hoped for, the evidence of things not seen."

Lingering Question 3: With religious freedom—or even the practice and priority of religious activity—being less of a current, contemporary factor in America than they were in past times, can the faith-seeking portion of the immigrant's motivational binary even be considered as an important reason for relocating permanently to the United States today?

Short Answer: Seeking faith opportunities and freedoms in the open society of America seems something we don't hear much about anymore. However, that thought has to co-exist with the

The Norwegian's Diary

reality of sub-groups such as theological student-expats streaming into American seminaries and universities for learning opportunities which they can theoretically take back to their home countries as ministers and teachers. On any kind of a mass basis, though, it is doubtful that great numbers of immigrants see America as a spiritual destination. Immigrants from a variety of world religions know that they will be free to practice their own faiths in pockets of likeminded adherents, but viewing America as anything more than a disunited secular state is somewhat of an antique myth. Much of the remigrant literature suggests that this may have always been the case as diaries and personal letters have often complained about a spiritual void existing at the center of American life: a void extending into all of the realms of culture, including media, politics, and business. America may be about many things, but any kind of a prevalent, monolithic spiritual place is not one of them. Indeed, if that place once existed, it doesn't anymore, even though, in the past, it endeavored to present itself as such.

CHAPTER THREE

The Mood of Destiny

THE YEAR 1897 SERVED as the opening year of Ollis Evenson's diary and functioned as a time of articulated destiny for an immigrant well on his way toward becoming an American citizen. At forty-seven, it was his seventeenth year in his adopted land, time enough for integrating himself into the prevailing mood, or *zeitgeist* if you will, of the country at that historical moment. But what was that zeitgeist at the close of the 19th century? We'll get to that in a moment.

Ollis tied the days, weeks, and months of 1897 together into a tightly bound package, offering thoughts seeming to emerge in step with the four seasons. In winter he wrote on January 24, "(Sunday) weather bitterly cold, stood 26 below zero at 7:30 A.M. Went to church." During spring, on May 20, he offered his birthday thoughts about turning forty-seven while reflecting nostalgically and geographically on his Norwegian place of birth. Then, his summer entry on July 4 featured his "mental commentary" on an America he couldn't readily recommend, at least privately in the anonymity of his own thoughts. And finally at the end of fall and in his anticipation of the following winter, he wrote that December 1 was a day of both "satisfaction" and "regret" as he officially received his American citizenship.

The Norwegian's Diary

> Went up for my citizenship paper, which I received with satisfaction, mingled with regret, as if every tie that bound me to my dear old Mother Norway had been severed. I know that I am still a descendant of the Vikings. I am yet a Son of Norway, and always will be to my dying day, although adopted as a foster child of this, the proudest Republic on Earth. I thank God for the land that bore me. I thank God for the land that adopted me. Lord, help me to be a good citizen of the latter, and to attain citizenship at last in the New Jerusalem above, for Thy Name's sake.

Security in church, nostalgia in remembering, frustration with American life, and the bittersweet experience of receiving citizenship, therefore, structured and summarized 1897 for Ollis. The reality of "citizenship," the recognition of "severed" ties, the emotional response to being an "adopted . . . foster child," the reference to seeing America as "the proudest" country on earth, and the personal, mystical vision of moving toward "the New Jerusalem above," revealed a soul in movement, in process, in transit, through necessary physical steps to a spiritual place beyond the temporal plane of an ordinary person's existence.

It has often been common for immigrants to have a destiny moment, similar to this one, on the day they sign their lives over to their new country. Even in our own day of dual citizenship, whereby individuals are free to retain legal status in their birth countries, the formal and ceremonial transition to a new country possesses a kind of permanence that suddenly makes one feel *locked* into a new place. Even if it's *the* place, where advantages outweigh disadvantages, the experience can be intimidating. It's as if larger, stronger forces are at work, stating formally to a new immigrant that "you belong to us now, know that, and know also that your old life as you knew it is gone forever."

That "citizenship paper," as Ollis called his official document, told the story. At the close of the century, it featured an arched *United States of America* logo rising above the words *Declaration of Intention*, a multi-digit number, name of state and court, and an arrangement of components establishing, verbally and pictorially, the mood of entering an all-encompassing sacred space. In this space beneath the arch, key personal details were housed: full name of the immigrant, age, occupation, skin color, complexion, height and weight, hair and eye color, and any distinguishing marks identifying the person. Place of birth, date of birth, current address, places of emigration and entry, vessel or carrier of transport, and last foreign address, followed. And lastly came the *serious* commitments: verbal renunciation of "all allegiance and fidelity to any foreign prince, potentate, state, or sovereignty" inclusive of name and title; declaration of not being an anarchist or a polygamist, and a vow "in good faith" to become "a citizen of the United States of America and to reside therein, so help me God." The document was then signed and dated by "the declarant" and an official of the court.

The finality of the experience was obviously not lost on Ollis, according to the diary. However, because that finality was not a completely embraced one, it was not actually *final*, and in this defining moment it was equally important for him to believe or imagine that a greater destiny, the "New Jerusalem above," should be included in his thinking. He was on his way there, to that higher place ultimately, a spiritual quest which allowed him to think of other commitments as temporary. Externally-imposed requirements to live a certain way, think a certain way, renounce "fidelity" to old "allegiances," adopt new philosophies, and to accept "in good faith" everything that defined American citizenship, "so help [him] God," framed only his present existence, not his permanent destiny. He could live with that.

Now, on to that late 19th century zeitgeist and how Ollis's thoughts might be seen to reside within the proverbial larger wheel of historical context that always turns the smaller wheel of an individual's private, personal life experiences.

First, allow me to take you into the nondescript, windowless classroom of the late Robert M. Figg III, who was a professor of American Literary Thought at my university during the mid/late-20th century. This was an educational era when long-established canons and contexts for understanding the cultural history of the

United States were still secure and difficult to challenge. His course was a hybrid of sorts, combining history, philosophy, and literature, and his period of focus was the second half of the 19th century. A portly southern eccentric of intense, wide-eyed enthusiasm, which occasionally intimidated students, animated his lectures, making them seem more like the sermons of a fiery southern fundamentalist preacher who was just a little crazy. He was not afraid to pound his podium to get his messages across.

Figg liked to begin his course by acting out scenes from Walt Whitman's seminal American classic, *Leaves of Grass*. Whitman's optimistic celebration of self, and his free verse associations of liberated spiritual and cognitive energy, took center stage with Figg seeming to inflate himself in front of the class, engaging students visually with Whitman's positive, poetic worldview. Later in the course, the professor became less emotion driven, more matter-of-fact, more cognitively objective, and more sarcastic as he sought to illustrate the practical realism of Mark Twain and Twain's contemporaries. Then, by course's end, Figg became somewhat mechanical, even machine-like, as he attempted to recreate the philosophical mood of the 19th century's closing years. His primary literary expression of those years was Theodore Dreiser's century-ending novel, *Sister Carrie*, an engaging but depressing story in which human freedom of choice took a back seat to deterministic life experiences confining people to inescapable destinies of general unhappiness. The novel's main characters who rose and fell in life not by their choices but by externally imposed forces, were persuasive. Had Figg been able to bring the sounds of steaming, clattering American factories, and street scenes of chaotic traffic fighting for survival in the civic corridors of Chicago and New York, he certainly would have done so.

"Do you see the great curve in American experience?" he bellowed just before the semester ended. "Do you see how things changed from one set of metaphors to quite another, one set of rules to a completely different one? It's so evident."

American determinism was the zeitgeist: a place of fixed futures, established orders, psychological laws, and natural

The Mood of Destiny

forces determining all outcomes of human experience and behavior. Whether seen and named as logical, theological, psychological, or physical (or eventually causal, biological, geographical, and environmental), each form of determined human existence was relevant to a Darwinian world of nature's dictatorial supremacy receiving increased acceptance during those late 19th century years.

Returning to Ollis Evenson's diary, moreover, and its 1897 zeitgeist context, we must recognize that even the basic thoughts of an ordinary person at the end of the 19th century should be understood to exist against this deterministic backdrop. Fate determined his destiny, according to this backdrop. Technology, geographical location, economic survival, family-rearing, media, employment requirements, and even church life, all played deterministic roles, keeping him in movement toward an ultimate destination. Ollis, of course, would not have articulated the reality of his life and world in so many words. There was no indication in the diary that secular philosophy occupied his thoughts, even though he tried to self-educate himself as much as possible. He very likely viewed himself, however, as framed and defined by lingering Calvinism and its religious worldview of an all-knowing God who predestined all things.

Calvinism as a relevant philosophy of life in America had been on the wane among the broad public for at least fifty years by that time, gradually replaced by an 1800s counter culture powerfully expressed during the 1850s literary explosion of works by Ralph Waldo Emerson and his contemporaries. Emerson's essays, Whitman's *Leaves of Grass*, *Walden* by Henry David Thoreau, *The Scarlet Letter* by Nathaniel Hawthorne, *Moby Dick* by Herman Melville, all published in that influential decade, functioned as liberators of transcendent ideas which evolved into other ideas and philosophies appreciated within America's emerging hybrid culture. This emergence also had the effect of relegating and confining Calvinism to America's churches, many of which maintained beliefs in the fall and depravity of human beings, unconditional grace for those elected by God to receive atonement through Jesus Christ's death and resurrection, and other fine points related to

The Norwegian's Diary

human free will as espoused by the immense body of discourses by French theologian, reformer, and pastor, John Calvin.

Ollis seemed a very good fit as a much-welcomed elect within Calvinism's comforting theology which predestined those chosen by God to receive eternally secure salvation, come what may in life. Any notions of the precariously lost salvation ideas resident within Calvinism's main opposing theology, Arminianism, which held that even strong believers could potentially be outed for reasons of persistent sin, were not a part of the picture here. For Calvinists, things might well get hard, disappointing, confusing, and terribly cruel in the earthly state, but with "citizenship at last in the New Jerusalem above," as Ollis stated, how bad could it be? His ultimate destiny was a sure thing if he "constantly cherished it in the bosom of [his] heart," as Calvin himself once wrote, and he would arrive there someday.

One additional Calvinist dictate, however, that had to be balanced with its theological promises, remained as Ollis's biggest challenge: perseverance. Could he persevere like a saint through all the obstacles life placed before him? His diary seemed to tell that story, as did other Nordic immigrant diaries of the period.

The thoughts put to paper by a Swedish-American immigrant, Iduna Bertel Field, for instance, offered a fairly matter-of-fact recounting of daily occurrences that included the weather, family activities, school events, holiday celebrations, and church happenings, proceeding as if ordered by external forces only rarely acknowledged. Born in the 1890s, she had been named after Idun, the mythical Norse goddess of youth and fertility who famously provided magical golden apples that reversed the aging process in other gods. Raised in rural Minnesota with six siblings, Field kept her diary in a Pillager, Minnesota farmhouse, only to be discovered a century later in the Nordic community of Decorah, Iowa. In her case, it wasn't the diary itself that provided great insights into the turn-of-the-century zeitgeist; it was rather the poetry she left behind that picked up where the diary left off. Thirty poems, stylistically reminiscent of Emily Dickinson, spoke of human stillness under the watchful eye of God, self-awareness

THE MOOD OF DESTINY

amid established patterns of immigrant life, being mourned while entering one's final place of rest in the grave, loneliness, identity, vanishing dreams, and life's fleeting moments before a God who answered all questions with his silence. "God's silence is His answer/The proof that He has heard/God's silence is His answer/His deep unspoken Word," she wrote. Field went on to take a degree at nearby Moorhead State University, taught school, and practiced journalism for the Decorah newspapers. But it was her poetry and lifelong interests in mental health—perhaps that of her fellow Nordic immigrants—that pressed her into co-founding a county-wide mental health association toward the end of her life.

A diary of greater substance was left by a Norwegian-American, Elizabeth Koren, who provided valuable insights into the immigrant's world during the years 1853–1855. Koren's diary seemed to suggest that her free will in choosing to emigrate diminished in stages as soon as she boarded the ship in the relative calm of Norwegian waters and was soon at sea. Once on open water, so many circumstances beyond one's control gave her the impression that her life as she had chosen it was now subject to the unpredictable whims of nature, and beings more powerful who made big decisions that determined the destinies of sojourning passengers. Sickness and death on the journey, the sudden drop-off of wind that stopped the ship's progress for many days, the perpetual motion of tossing waves once the wind returned, and an endless monotony that was unshakable by worship services, book reading, or onboard social activities that couldn't relieve the tedium, were all part of the external, controlling forces encapsulating the emigrants. This amounted to stage one of feeling gripped and shuffled like chess pieces across the mysterious board of an unknown future.

Stage two began with the relief of finally arriving in America, but was soon followed by the chaotic disembarking process in New York City, which prompted comments from Koren like, "The Americans' taste for being amused by violence and cruelty was obvious." Stage three involved a long, freezing land and lake journey through the American Midwest, followed by the arrival at Koren's destination: Iowa, which had recently become a state.

The Norwegian's Diary

She celebrated her journey's end but confided to the diary that "I soon wished myself home again, I cannot deny it" and "Last year I began the new year . . . with roses in my hair [while] this year I am sitting [alone] in this bare room." She further confided about having the most painful night dreams of her home in Norway with no possibility of returning "to the scenes" embedded in memory. "Melancholy" became her newly imposed emotional state as she reflected on having exchanged "church bells" and "holy days" for "one desolate prairie after another" where "it is no use to regret" her former life which had "now vanished." Sinking to her lowest level of melancholia and despair, she wrote, somewhat metaphorically perhaps, "I am very tired . . . and it is always late in the evening now." As the diary ended only three years after it began, it is not known how long the processes of acclimation and adaptation to her American life took for Koren. In surviving personal letters, and a forward to one of the diary's reprints years later, however, she does seem to have accepted the life that had been given her personally, domestically, and spiritually. Did she choose it, or was it chosen for her? Many 19th century immigrants told a similar story of acceptance, some with a heavy dose of stoicism induced by the recognition which, like the famous "Serenity Prayer" decades later, urged them "to accept that which cannot be changed."

Still another Nordic diary, assembled in pieces beneath a fictional narrative self-published by Roger Andersen, speaks through diary fragments left by Andersen's Norwegian-American grandfather whose immigration journey began at sixteen and in the early years of the 20th century. The engine-powered sea crossing was, of course, much faster and less-affected by nature than the months-long sailing ship voyages of Koren's time, so outside of a briefly enforced quarantine caused by a passenger's eye infection there didn't seem to be much that might have brought questions about free will into the experience. Upon arrival at Ellis Island, however, the shock of reality pressed this immigrant into survival mode created by the needs for quick employment, money, and a place to live. Difficult work on a tobacco farm for low pay followed, as did bad food, loneliness, and other factors that led to a hard, unhappy period of time. Work at a rock quarry didn't seem much better, but it did allow him to save enough money to pay off his debt to creditors who had paid for the ocean passage. Then, new job after new job seemed to dictate his progression to marginally better situations, and as he bounced and rebounded geographically from east to west and south, a life of determined—some might even say *predetermined*—progress defined his immigrant life. He fell in love, married, had children and later grandchildren, attended church, revisited Norway, and lived happily, at least until his wife, Rikke, fell victim to successive heart attacks and died. "Rikke is gone forever," he wrote in the diary. "I feel terribly lonely . . . life is closing in on me . . . I feel old . . . my journey is over . . . I look forward to going home," he added.

Thoughts of "going home" echo throughout Ollis Evenson's diary, whether home meant "the land that bore" him, "the land that adopted" him, or even "the New Jerusalem above," as he wrote upon receiving his American citizenship on December 1, 1897. *Home* was a precarious triangle, though, of past, present, and future for an immigrant whose choices were limited, whose survival pressures were immense, and whose life experiences reflected the deterministic mood of that moment in history. Many immigrants to America would have agreed with such destiny comments, inclusive of predestination arguments, though some disagreed vehemently based on the notion that all humans have free will granted by a loving God who allows us to determine our own lives in a world created for freedom, possibility, and prosperity. It was a conversation punctuated by all the emotional investment and theological pathos of the time. No wonder historians Jon Gjerde and Carlton C. Qualey could say in their book, *Norwegians in Minnesota*, that some immigrants "argued predestination in the saloons, with their tongues . . . and settled it in the alley with their fists."

Lingering Question 4: What range of emotions animated discussions of free will in generations of immigrants to America, and what roles did they play in splintering religious believers into social units such as church denominations, while others left church and faith completely because of them?

Short Answer: Believing in free will that afforded human beings with an all-encompassing liberty to craft and establish their own personal life narratives was, and is, a welcome and happy thought for many people. Even in the presence of a cosmic overseer who watches what we do and who we are, we can know that oversight does not mean control or power over our choices. We're free to determine our own chosen destinies, and even free to make our own failures on which we can build the associated successes we desire, which is as American as warm apple crisp with vanilla ice cream. Anything less than a belief in free will seems an affront to how we want our life courses to be realized. Yet, some might say that predetermined lives and a determined world of natural processes can also be a happy form of existence if we place our trust in a higher power who knows far better than we know what is best for ourselves and our world. Such security—*eternal security*, according to the Calvinists—allows us to "rest in the Lord and wait patiently for him," according to Psalm 37:7. Fear is eliminated, replaced by love, devotion, delight, and other positive abstractions from that same psalm. Correspondingly, anything less than a belief in God's ordering of all things is just wrong and ignorant of obvious evolving processes of a naturalistic world and universe. Be humble before the higher power, by this view, and don't think you have more self-determinative power than you actually have. Strong emotions emerged from both sets of beliefs and values held by immigrants. No surprise, therefore, at the fist-fighting metaphor provided by Gjerde and Qualey.

CHAPTER FOUR

American Immigrant Ecclesia

Dear Christopher,

Before I get more into your ancestor's church life as an immigrant, can I tell you a little about my own *church* story?

My personal immigrant *ecclesia* experience will, I believe, illuminate one of two major reasons I felt compelled to revisit Ollis's diary so many years after finding it at that Saint Paul garage sale. I now strongly identify with its church component, and indeed with immigrants who have found faith communities to play an important role in navigating the move from the country of one's birth to the country of one's choosing. The simple act of going to church can function as fellowship for the lonely or as a kind of sacramental narrative for those seeking something deeper: a centering stability which serves as an antidote to naturally occurring immigrant dislocation.

I'll start by saying how surprised I was at my sudden need for becoming part of a church once I had settled into Portuguese life. In the United States, I had frankly grown quite comfortable in never attending a church. I didn't like it, felt I didn't need it, and didn't want to sacrifice the few quiet hours provided by the peaceful weekly interval of time known as Sunday morning. I could use that quietness to pray, meditate, read the Bible, read Thomas Merton or Henri Nouwen, listen to recorded hymns or Gregorian chant, or simply enjoy a peaceful breakfast, on my own, without joining some repetitive, collective experience of contemporized religion. I'd had enough of that over the course of my life. Enough corporate rituals, sermons, God-talk, testimonies, fellowship, collection plate passing, fundraising pleas, missionary reports, banquets, Christmas pageants, church picnics, and rallies. Simply enough.

Much of that changed, though, after I immigrated.

I attended my wife's Portuguese *igreja* for a few weeks, though the language barrier was insurmountable, disallowing anything beyond a very basic appreciation for unfamiliar cultural worship norms. I needed English as my religious currency, so began to explore the few English-language faith communities in and around Lisbon. A couple of Anglican churches held possibilities, though the one closest to the house was fronted by a huge cemetery of mossy grave stones that would have to be passed through each week before entering the otherwise beautiful cathedral, and the other was an hour-long train ride away. There were also a few ultra-contemporary, guitar-and-drum places operating in rented storefronts, led by hip seminary grads in stretch-trousers and sneakers. I respected their appeal to young locals and digital nomads spread across popular, contemporary Lisbon, but the cool, entertainment-driven style reminded me too much of the same in so many American churches, so I didn't go back.

When, with my wife, we found a local Church of Scotland across cobblestoned, antique Lisbon, we felt immediately at home. Stopping for breakfast in the nearby Museu de Arte Antiga, we then followed the cobblestones up a steep hill to the church and entered as thousand-year-old hymns echoed in a vintage, stained glass sanctuary. We wanted this. We wanted history and tradition. These factors engaged my historian wife, and because I was familiar with Scottish rites and culture from having lived there for a few years, we agreed that this was our place. In the ensuing weeks, I surprised myself yet again by wishing to be more than a visionless spectator and welcomed opportunities to become part of the church's mission as an elder who might even preach on occasion. When these opportunities presented themselves, I said yes to becoming involved, risking the loss of a more private religious life in favor of lay ministry in this small, struggling faith community. Traditional churches everywhere are dying these days, and committing oneself to a diminishing shadow from the past can be hard to do. You might still have hopes and dreams for reviving the object that casts the shadow, but if you're realistic at all, you can't have expectations.

In any case, Christopher, that's a capsulized version of my immigrant ecclesia story.

Immigration, especially as we age, has a way of getting us to reflect on things we once found important, even if over the course of living in the familiarity of our origins, we lost sight of them, buried them, or simply let them slip away into nothingness. A time comes, however, when, in the unfamiliarity of our immigrant lives, we ache to revive those former things, and the only question is *why*. It's easy enough to attribute the phenomenon, superficially, to nostalgia for the past. It's more insightful to consider the power of *attachment theory* and the idea that over the life course we eventually return to an idealized image of our early years and how we made even a child's sense of the world around us. We attended church and Sunday school, and so we return to them eventually for comfort, security, and an awareness that one day we're going to die. But it's more than either nostalgia or attachment, I believe. It's also about an external force that gently pulls us back into our true selves and *the word that was hidden in our heart*, to paraphrase Psalm 119: 11. To further paraphrase John 10:28, *nothing and no one shall pluck us away* from that force, the evidence being our return to spiritual things initiated by the all-encompassing Christ within us. This can happen, of course, even if we never leave our origins in the first place, but it becomes more evident and pronounced when we're a long way from them, as in an immigrant situation.

I have wondered, moreover, if something like this had happened with your ancestor, Ollis. He was well into middle age when he started to commit his own ecclesia thoughts to his diary. Was he revealing and reliving latent memories and desires from his past, pre-emigration life in Norway where almost everyone had been reared in Lutheran social and theological traditions? And did he find, like I did as a mainline believer from America who emigrated to Europe, that these long-past attachments suddenly or gradually resurfaced in the unfamiliarity of his new life as an immigrant? Did he need his past so powerfully that the only way of reviving it was through the experience of secure, organized religion in his new country? Or was it that mysterious Christ-force within his heart pulling him back? Whatever motives drove him into that craved security at about fifty years old, he expressed them through habitual acts of participatory church involvement that guided him through the challenges of his life in the volatile America of his time.

A typical week in any year of the diary had Ollis leading a prayer meeting on Sunday evening, participating in a midweek evangelistic service, conducting the music at a multi-hour funeral on Saturday, and preaching a lay sermon the following Sunday morning. He also found time to arrange hymns for the church choir and for on-the-spot counseling requests from church members, ministerial tasks which were accomplished amid his own family responsibilities and the excruciating work-life of a turn-of-the-century tradesperson. The diary:

> January 30, 1898: (Sunday) We went to church, and Rev. Wilson having a bad cold and sore throat, I took the Pulpit and preached to the congregation as well as I could. In the afternoon Otto Brack came to our house wanting me to give him lessons in voice culture.

Ollis felt that old Calvinistic urge to be a lay preacher, and as this was a direct call from God himself nothing was going to compromise the role of standing before a group of listeners waiting for the dissemination of inspired words. Repeatedly, he wrote of being thrust into the pulpit in his ordained pastor's absence, delighted to feel "that God was very near to me the whole time" (Feb. 21, 1897); or to administer Holy Communion. His diary entry on February 16, 1913 yielded a snippet of that story:

Being a lay preacher only, it certainly was a most novel experience for me to be called upon to administer the Lord's Supper to my Brothers and Sisters. It was the first and no doubt the last time in my life to render such an exalted service in the Church.

That Ollis's pastor was willing to violate ordination codes in this way showed how much personal faith he had in his Norwegian-American layman.

Immigrant lay ministers had a colorful history. They often functioned as the right-hand servants of their ordained, overworked clergy for whom ministerial burnout was a common problem. I learned a lot about this from having once edited a journal for church leaders during a brief, post-university moment. Counseling centers, therapeutic retreats, and hasty career departures were common among contemporary ministers, though in Ollis's time they were rare, precipitating a need for the enlistment of lay people. The first Scandinavian lay ministers were described as rugged and hardy, like Old Testament prophets. They preached repentance and salvation, and many possessed sharp intellects despite their lack of any formal education. Some were *Haugeans*, who vigorously followed the pious Norwegian reformer Hans Nielsen Hauge in bringing renewal to Norwegian Christians within and without the Norwegian Lutheran state church, expressing their rebellious dislike of authority figures, formally educated officials, and anyone who fostered class-conscious, top-down systems of governance. They fit well, therefore, into the American immigrant ecclesia of the 19th century, confronting and debating formally-trained ministers whom they sometimes judged as *papistical*.

Although Ollis used that caustic, anti-Catholic insult, *papistical*, several times in the diary—perhaps, though, not with venomous intent—he never said a thing about being a Haugean. His lay ministry, rather, seemed more modest and less volatile, possibly being more in the tradition of Elling Eilsen, Claus Clausen, and Paul Andersen, all spiritually directed Norwegian-American lay voices from the 1800s. Eilsen, a blacksmith by trade who also farmed and worked as a carpenter, brought spiritual leadership to the Fox River community of Norwegians in Illinois and was said to know the entire Bible by heart. Clausen nurtured the faith community of Norwegian-American farmers in the once-Potawatomi indigenous settlement of Muskego, Wisconsin. Andersen, a disciple of Eilsen, fought against physical illness and the death of his only child to preach a simple, direct Gospel wherever he felt led by God. Ollis would seem to have been comfortable in the presence of these laity.

Confession: I wrongly stated in my original *Books & Culture* article that Ollis had been a likely member of a Methodist-Episcopal church in Saint Paul, Minnesota, only to revise that conjecture now, twenty-five years later. After finding Ollis's diary, I had many conversations about it with my then father-in-law, Richard, the son of Norwegian immigrants who had settled in a farming community on the flat, earth-hued landscapes of northern Iowa. Richard was a man of deep faith who had intentionally departed from his Norwegian Lutheran background to become part of a non-denominational missionary fellowship in Bloomington, Minnesota. This fellowship was alive and visionary, he said, a marked departure from the stagnant, state Lutheranism originating in Norway. He never regretted making the change.

One day as we were discussing Ollis's diary, Richard suddenly stated in his wavering voice, compromised by Parkinson's Disease, that there was no way Ollis could have been traditionally Lutheran. His zeal as a layman suggested some kind of *low-church* involvement rather than the *high-church* Lutheranism of set-in-stone church polity. Since we didn't know his exact denomination, we began to speculate. We crossed off Baptists and Presbyterians—I can't remember why exactly—but opened ourselves up to Methodists and Episcopalians, each of whom had a long history in Saint Paul. In the days ahead, some further reading at the Sons of Norway culture center, and a Minneapolis library, had me considering that Ollis may have been part of the Methodist-Episcopal church, which had moved to the Twin Cities from Chicago on newly-constructed rail lines a little before his immigration. The anti-elite, countercultural, and evangelistic MEC churches seemed as good a fit as any for Ollis, so that is where we left things. But I'll say this now: guessing a person's denomination during Ollis's time is a bit like playing the vintage detective board game, *Clue*, in which you're never really sure if it was Colonel Mustard or Mrs. Peacock, Professor Plum or Miss Scarlet, who committed the crime.

So, I was wrong, Christopher, as several *experts* in *Books & Culture's* audience informed me. They were right.

To wit: I am now persuaded to believe that Ollis had remained a Lutheran, though in the context of American evangelical Lutheranism which aligned more closely with his religious life. The sum of his actions and beliefs, his piety and reform, his evangelism and lay leadership, and his need of an outlet for the peculiar Lutheran confessionalism committed to his diary, probably anchored him in the United Norwegian Lutheran Church of America or one of its close evangelical variants active during the years of the diary. By doing so, he would remain loyal to his ethnic roots while simultaneously becoming *free* as an American immigrant whose ecclesia facilitated his growth toward an equally forward-looking perspective on faith and life. I'll maintain, however, that he was the somewhat unusual *crypto-Calvinist* as a Lutheran who believed deep in his soul that God had pre-ordained his steps, established his present life, held him fast in ministry and perseverant living, and in all ways determined his future as a servant obedient to his ultimate master.

Ancestral records state that Niels Olaus "Ollis" Evenson, born in Norderhov, Buskerud Norway on May 20, 1850 to Even Nelson and Sophia Christiansdatter, died on July 18, 1928 in the Norwegian Evangelical Lutheran community of Saint Peter, Minnesota. Mother Sophia lived from 1822–1903, and Father Even from 1822–1900. Births and deaths followed, extended as branches throughout a large family tree of descendants and others connected to the tree through marriage, in an ordered pattern as though established and sustained by an external, unseen presence operating beyond the veil of human recognition. It was the story of the Evenson genealogy, but it could have been any family's pattern of existence whose sojourn through life was visible and appreciable.

The Norwegian's Diary

For Ollis, being born into Norwegian Lutheranism, expanding into an American Lutheran experience that was familiar but more consistent with New World freedoms, and finally ending battle in a Minnesota Lutheran stronghold, his life must have seemed enveloped in a sacramental narrative needed and enjoyed but inescapable in its all-encompassing power. Destiny has different ways of making its presence known.

Lingering Question 5: How much does the viability and sustainability of the American church owe to legions of dislocated, vulnerable immigrants whom, at least during this insecure stage of their lives, craved an experience of hope not found in any other place?

Short Answer: After long and often perilous journeys by sea and over land, immigrants to America often arrived hand-in-hand with an unwanted companion: fear. Many thought their journey was over, but in fact it was just beginning. The lucky ones had people to receive them, but most faced unknown futures and a realization that they were suddenly, hopelessly alone; adrift on landscapes, lakes, and rivers where dangers and hostilities were more the rule than the exception. A hope narrative awaited, however, in the form of believing, worship communities established by missionaries and visionary ministers who ran interference routes to even the remotest locations on the expanding continent, waiting to serve the psychologically meandering masses. The best of these communities offered authentic spiritual direction; the worst of them lived to exploit and corrupt, leaving the arrivals in worse shape than that which stoked their uncertainties in the first place. Vulnerable immigrants were, moreover, easy prey for the bad places, whereas the better, genuine, faith-seeking environments offered avenues for lay participation benefitting the immigrants themselves and building strong, enduring worship communities. Many great churches of all denominations emerged from this matrix and are still in operation today. If they are hemorrhaging members, as many are, it may be safe to say that losing the flow of vulnerable immigrants into their sanctuaries plays at least a partial role in rapidly diminishing fellowships across America.

CHAPTER FIVE

Mercy Please

PERSONAL DIARIES HAVE DIFFERENT ways of telling, and adding to, a diarist's story.

Long entries sometimes offer a complete picture of something that happened in the diarist's life, while short, repeating entries spread over time but devoted to a single event or theme can be even more thorough in revealing a beginning, middle, and ending of an important event.

Then, there are the brief stand-alone entries that articulate something so traumatic that nothing more is said, ever, which would offer a more complete telling of what happened. They're the proverbial tips of the iceberg in which the great bulk of understanding lies beneath the surface. The details, the cause-and-effect particulars, and everything else that produced the backstory stay submerged, and we're left to make educated guesses about the nature and extent of what it was all about.

An entry like this occurred for Ollis on August 28, 1900 when he painfully mentioned his participation in the delivery of his father to a local mental hospital.

He wrote,

> Father was this day committed to the Rochester Hospital for [the] Insane. As I, personally, had to figure prominently in the commitment, I hope and pray that I may be

spared from performing a similar duty again. Oh—it was an awful hard thing to do! Lord have mercy upon us all!

Nothing more was said as silence replaced any further explanation of this excruciating situation. Ancestry records state that the father, *Even*, died at some point that same year, though whether or not his time simply had come, or if the commitment itself had led somehow to his death, was never reported in any known obituary or by Ollis himself in the diary.

Any critical guesswork here associated with this diary entry is just that: a guess. There is not much to support further explanation of what happened, why it happened, and what it meant. However, as the linking of immigrants to mental illness, especially among Europeans moving to America during the 19th and early 20th centuries, is such an important subject in immigrant literature, it seems worth an effort to shed some light. We have no idea if Ollis's father was simply a common victim of senile dementia in his final years, or if there was more to the story. Were we to grasp a larger recognition of immigrant mental illness, though, we have much to go on that might be seen to apply to the difficult journeys made by immigrants during and before Ollis's time. Many struggled to maintain sanity throughout the transition from their places of origin to that of new, unfamiliar lives where everything had to be learned, relearned, hurdled, and accepted.

Even today that can be the case.

Anu Partanen's 2016 memoir, *The Nordic Theory of Everything: In Search of a Better Life*, for instance, spends ample time discussing anxiety, depression, obstacles to happiness, negativity, divorce, mental illness, personal stability, pessimism, angst, imbalance, and suicide, all in the context of Nordic immigration to America. Early in the memoir, she writes about "anxiety spreading through me, and no amount of reasoning could stop the physical wave of dread . . . . I felt alone and in trouble." Later, she references an erosion of personal optimism while witnessing a urine-soaked homeless man, helpless and alone in a subway station while others passed by in their seemingly productive, successful lives. And by the end of the memoir, Partanen leaves us wondering about "the lack of true security" in America and how it is replaced by "your own personal well-being bubble" constructed through a peculiar American calculus of superficial addictions like fast food and tv binges with deeper attempts to survive through therapies such as yoga and meditation.

But again, how can any of this be compared to the mental states of Nordic immigrants a century ago, even if ethnicity of mind is a relevant measure? We need a different story—indeed, a different analytical and contextual framework—that goes back a hundred-plus years to even begin to comprehend what might have led to an immigrant's commitment to a turn-of-the-century American insane asylum.

We would likely have to begin with the emigrant journey itself: the transition.

A recent contribution to the European literature of 19th century emigrant journeys to America by ship is 2021's *The Coffin Ship: Life and Death at Sea during the Great Irish Famine*, by Cian T. McMahon. It's an Irish emigrant story, of course, so how much of it can reasonably apply to Norway's emigrants, other than the fact that both countries were literally drained by their escaping populations via the Atlantic Ocean in the 1800s? Also, it explores an earlier time, 1845–55, decades before Ollis's emigration in 1880, though we don't know when his father made the journey. Did the parents travel with their sons? Did they leave Norway earlier or later? We simply do not know. I am guessing from the diary that they followed Ollis and his brother Charles, whom after emigrating themselves possibly encouraged their parents to make their way across the ocean and thereby reunite the family in America.

In any event, the parents' journey would not have been an easy one because no one's 19th century emigrant sojourn was easy.

A staggering amount of physical and psychological preparation for the experience was the first step, according to McMahon. Deciding whether to go or stay put, leaving loved ones who stayed behind, and preparing to deal with difficult co-passengers were as much a part of preparation as raising the necessary cash and negotiating onboard provisions like bedding and cooking utensils.

Mercy Please

Packing clothing suitable for extremes of weather, undergoing required medical exams, and securing one's baggage before and after boarding, added to the anxiety. Then, once on board, there were the challenges of building relationships with trustworthy co-passengers, protecting against theft and violence, even from crew members, and finding a way of fitting oneself into the tiny berth spaces which remained small even after steamships replaced smaller sailing vessels. Personal *morality* space was a further concern, in that context, especially for women and girls subjected to sexual violence, according to many sources.

Life at sea was probably some combination of excitement and dread for most emigrants. Vistas of the open ocean, healing mists inhaled by asthma sufferers, and vivid sunsets spreading across the western sky—the *destination* sky—hopefully balanced the onslaught of violent storms, motion sickness, and ill health which could spread to everyone enclosed within the ship's tight interior quarters. Then, there were the ever-present, death-at-sea threats with infectious diseases doing most of the damage, inflicting harms that made instances of malnutrition and exhaustion seem lesser issues to worry about. Typhus was the main killer on emigrant ships, but cholera was a faster killer, sometimes taking its victims down within a few diarrhea-explosive, dehydration-draining hours. By Ollis's and his parents' time, emigrant ships were required by law to employ resident medical staff, but fatal diseases still killed, and all that was left were the resulting horrors of at-sea burials. Sometimes, emigrant priests and ministers provided comfort through prayer and Bible reading for demoralized passengers, but when they weren't onboard or available, anxiety incubated like a virus itself until the ship reached port. At the receiving port, moreover, the anxiety may have diminished in the excitement of walking into a new life, though that was true only for the extremely fortunate emigrants who had people and places waiting for them. For the less fortunate ones, one set of anxieties were simply replaced by another set that may well have included predatory agents and brokers looking to make fast cash through promoting dishonest opportunities and enterprises.

The Norwegian's Diary

Loneliness and insecurity upon arrival was a stark reality that many arriving ship passengers to America never got over, according to immigration historians. It often began at the moment of separation from onboard friendships formed among emigrants trying to cope with miseries of the journey. Trying to stick together on shore was then compromised by being pulled apart by customs processing and the scattering of emigrants scrambling for employment and a place to live. Many spoke no English at all, and without money drained from their savings, the last of which went to expenses of the transoceanic journey, the challenges of finding a way to survive were both immediate and enduring. Luck might give them a fighting chance in the extreme working conditions of the capitalist economy, but falling apart physically, emotionally, and psychologically was always possible. Thus, any suggestion that the realities of *arrival-shock* had something to do with later struggles involving mental disease and even insanity need to be taken seriously.

Ellis Island – A People's History, by the Polish journalist Malgorzata Szejnert, tells the brutal story of immigrants marginalized upon arrival by poverty, illness, cognitive inadequacy, various forms of neurosis, and behaviors officially judged as dangerous. From the early 1890s to well into the early 20th century, statistics cited by Szejnert of people entering at the Port of New York include 16.6 million total arrivals, 610,000 refusals of entry, 80,000 impaired by mental and physical maladies, 16,000 stowaways, 13,600 who were functionally illiterate, 8,000 who were rejected for morality issues, and 300 judged as subversive. This was the story of Ellis Island only, with the numbers and arrival stories at other ports of entry such as Baltimore, Boston, Philadelphia, New Orleans (and the Canadian ports of Halifax and Quebec, Ollis's likely entry point) not included. "Lunatics and idiots," "insane persons," people who arrived with "attacks of insanity" in their personal histories, and "imbeciles and persons mentally or physically defective . . . being of a nature which may affect the ability of such aliens to earn a living" were cited in the various American Immigration Acts commencing in 1891 and their revised versions that followed.

Mercy Please

Vulnerable immigrants falling into "the hands of the enemy" was how one career employee, interviewed by Szejnert, described what she had witnessed over the years of her employment.

"Travel exhaustion" was "the hard part" of determining the complex mental states of arrivals, according to one medical professional, a situation made worse by additional travel which began with deportation for unfortunates. One Nathan Cohen, described by Szejnert as "a Jewish wanderer" and "a mysterious figure" had emigrated from a small town in Russia, traveling first to Brazil, then to America, where he married and started a business. After the business failed and his wife left him for another man, his abilities to remember and even to speak deserted him, resulting in his commitment to a mental hospital in Baltimore. Prior to his insanity diagnosis, he had been deported to Brazil, back to America, then to Russia, again to the US, back to Brazil, and yet again to America where he ended up a Jewish charity case. Another story involved an Italian girl in her teens who arrived speaking a dialect no one at Ellis Island could understand. Failing to answer questions she couldn't understand, she was sent to a hospital where a male doctor tested her reflexes by tapping her knees and touching her spine, producing a reaction so violent that an observer said it "was the cruelest case I ever witnessed on the island." Within weeks, the girl became "a raving maniac," said the observer, "although she had been sound and normal when she arrived at Ellis Island."

At different times, some arriving immigrants were described as "mentally defective," "mentally backward," "feeble minded," "parasites" who had "no purpose of becoming productive," and as "lumps of poisonous leaven." One official is cited by Szejnert as believing that "mental illness and mental disability" were "hereditary and . . . therefore beyond the power of society to prevent." Such was the state of immigrant mental diagnosis near the turn of the 20th century where in New York hospitals, according to Szejnert's sources, nearly half of all mental illness cases were from outside America yet outsiders made up only a quarter of the general population. Deportation and even plans for eugenic treatments were the solutions, some believed, even as others viewed such actions as a way of *sinning* "against the men and women they've driven to despair by dividing families, condemning relatives to isolation, and ruining lives," Szejnert summarizes.

Remigrant literature also has much to say about immigrant mental illness pertaining to travelers who returned to their countries of birth after being unable or unwilling to adapt to America's harsh conditions. The "boomerang" mentality driven by emotional pain, failure, insanity, isolation, loneliness, pathological nostalgia, restlessness, and psychological trauma, as explored by Susan J. Matt in *Homesickness – An American History*, involved a total collapse of adaptability for some immigrants who were literally kept alive by their hope of returning home. "Many felt homesick their whole lives," she writes, if they were unable to remigrate. Adaptability required constant courage which these immigrants could never seem to muster except perhaps through living "artificially" by clutching onto the memories of one's past life.

"'My heart is constricted, and I begin to run like a madman till the tears stream from my eyes,'" Matt quotes a Russian-American immigrant prohibited from being homeward bound. The "pathetic insanity of nostalgia" affected many who had become prone to idealizing the past and regretful of their personal losses of "imagined order and purity," she adds. Finding a new self in places where they had no living essence of ethno-geographical history or cultural familiarity eluded them with the looming possibility of ending up a part of "asylum populations." Asylums became the alternative for individuals who might have found temporary anesthetizing relief to their suffering from "the cultural products of capitalism," but whose deep psychological pain remained permanently fixed. Suicide was another way out, and as mentioned by Matt, suicide reports contextualized by homesickness among immigrants became an oft-reported story in newspapers of the era.

Round-Trip to America – The Immigrants Return to Europe, 1880–1930 by Mark Wyman suggests that some Nordic remigrants were stuck on the idea that in America *freedom* wasn't real freedom. It was more a matter of adhering to a narrowminded *Americanism* of flag worship and platitudes of "American way" thinking and behaving. Unable to adapt to this mentality while at the same time being pressured to leave what they interpreted as a truer understanding of human society—the society of their nostalgia-conditioned past—nurtured their desire to remigrate. Even though other remigrants said that living in America had opened them up to a larger view of life and the world, they too wanted the simpler life available in their countries of origin. They might never again experience the forward-looking, innovative life of westward journeys to a bold new destiny, but they would be more satisfied by regaining an in-tact soul built upon their eastern foundations.

Echoing some of these themes in *The Promise of America: A History of the Norwegian-American People*, Odd Lovoll contextualizes the topic of immigrant suffering with forays into Norwegian-American literature, the "force" of which came from "preserving Norwegian culture" and "protecting the ancestral heritage," he argues. Mental illness, assimilation problems, longing for home, insecurities produced by excessive mobility, persistent idealization of the past, and other "distresses" resounded between the covers of books written by Norwegian Americans. First-generation immigrants bore most of the conflict in stories, and one consistent portrayal of characters' pain centered on children trying "to escape from their Norwegian background," thereby becoming rootless, adrift, and psychologically distant from honored traditions "of the fatherland," Lovoll writes. Playing important roles in "building the American nation" through "safeguarding" one's traditions was paramount, and "'a people without traditions is doomed," he quotes a character portrayal by one author. "'Strangers we are to the people we left, and strangers we are to the people we came to,'" also quoted by Lovoll, seems strikingly relevant to the emotional conflicts felt by all immigrants to America, not only Norwegian ones.

No doubt, this loneliness of not truly belonging anywhere contributed to another issue documented by Lovoll: the high rate of "drunkenness" among Norwegian-American immigrants. Alcoholism itself was so common in Norway until at least the mid-19th century, according to Lovoll, that some Norwegians actually used emigration "as the only way out" after losing everything to the bottle. Finding their way to America where they wouldn't have to deal with anti-alcohol pietism emerging in Norway at that time, at least seemed like a reasonable alternative to unwanted, reform-driven social pressure to dry out. Upon settling into their new land of "wretched" work conditions, "destructive materialism," and "tragic patterns" of immigrant life, however, those with consumptive intent found themselves thrust into the after-hours "saloon culture" of "fights and moral decay," Lovoll states. I inherited first-hand accounts of this phenomenon from my one-time Norwegian-American mother-in-law, Mary Ann, who told many stories of her father who had fallen into that culture. As immigrants to the prairies of South Dakota, she spoke simultaneously of her mother, Bergliot, who often had to intercept her husband's paychecks before he could blow them in the local saloons.

Even though instances of criminal behavior were low among Scandinavians in Minneapolis and St. Paul, according to Lovoll, public "drunkenness and disorder" were high. Prostitution was also a factor among Scandinavian women compromised by financial insecurity, and suicides received frequent mentions in Norwegian-American newspapers. "Stress and emotional strain [were] revealed in the statistics of patients in mental institutions," Lovoll concludes, with the very common truth within all immigrant cultures in America: insanity was much higher there than elsewhere. "Empirical evidence" as to why this was and perhaps still is the case might be lacking, though the anecdotal evidence paints an indelible image of how difficult it has always been to leave a place of familiarity for one of unknown, unanticipated factors, no matter the accompanying rewards of the move.

We'll never know the exact reasons behind Ollis's plea for mercy on that late-August day in 1900, but we can certainly imagine. Perhaps they were a similar set of reasons that led Iduna Field to co-establish her mental health association in Decorah, Iowa. While less emotionally subjective than Ollis's regrets over losing his father, she did seem to be consumed by regular observations of town residents who stole, seethed, fought, and even attempted to murder, thereby exhibiting clear signs of mental illness that caused her to do what she could to better understand troubled minds. And her poetry offered stark lyrical forays into deep, dark recesses of the mind, forays visited upon her fellow immigrants and undoubtedly herself that not only diagnosed root problems of the immigrant experience but also the lingering after-effects of unaddressed and untreated suffering. In one poem seeming to ponder the "strange refrain" that follows human loneliness in a person, she wrote, "Loneliness too long endured becomes a song/It sings itself out and then it is gone/but a strange refrain lives on/a strange refrain lives on . . . ." Perhaps some sort of strange refrain had been observed by a troubled Ollis Evenson in his father, leading to the painful institutional committal on that unfortunate day in 1900.

August 28, 1900 offered clear skies and temperatures in the upper 70s, lows in the 50s, across the entire state of Minnesota. President William McKinley occupied the White House in Washington, DC. Helen and John were the most popular names given to babies, with Anna and William coming in second place. The Rochester Hospital for the Insane was in its twenty-first year of operation, having opened in 1879 as the Minnesota Inebriate Hospital specializing in the treatment of alcoholism. Its red-brick structure featured a minaret-like administrative tower with pillars and a metallic dome on top in the center of the campus with patient wards spreading out at ground level on both sides, and there was plenty of land space for further construction. Female and male patients worked in a sewing room, a tailor shop, a power station, kitchen, bakery, and laundry room to support the residents. A large farm, also staffed mostly by patients, produced food from crops and dairy cows for the community. Patients transferred in from the Hospital for the Insane located in St. Peter, Minnesota, first because of overcrowding, next because a fire burned the St. Peter facility to the ground. The Rochester Hospital for the Insane shortened its name to the Rochester State Hospital and was ultimately demolished in later years, an event reported by local newspapers. But on this day, in this turn-of-the-century year, a grieving, fifty-year-old Norwegian-American man placed his father in the care of nurses and doctors attired in clinical white, as he then walked away pleading for God's mercy.

Lingering Question 6: What are the possibilities that the immense existence of poor mental health among long-ago immigrants to America produced an *instinct* of sorts predisposing current generations of Americans to instances of compromised mental health?

Short Answer: When Charles Darwin was observing animal species in the Galapagos Islands during the 1830s, he remarked on how tame the birds seemed. Without a fear of humans, as a result of their geographical isolation, they could be lifted onto a finger even while sipping water to quench their thirst. Darwin's conclusion was that tameness could be seen as hereditary over the course of generations and ultimately an instinct. While it is difficult to compare birds to humans, studies of human behavior becoming instinctive in just a few generations seems relevant. While mental health proper doesn't appear to be on most lists of human instincts, emotions such as anger, envy, fear, jealousy, and rivalry are. Is it possible, therefore, to view mental health as a collection of emotions that have evolved into something like instinct in humans, and to locate its points of origin in large phenomena such as immigration which was laden with challenges to healthy mental behavior? This would have been a question to place before the Nordic-American immigrant, Iduna Bertel Field, relevant to her interests in immigrant mental health and her role in co-founding Iowa's Winneshiek County Mental Health Association, and later as president of the Iowa Mental Health Association; or, to anyone who has studied the mental health of dislocated immigrants to America who suffered throughout the transition from one known-life experience to an unknown one.

CHAPTER 6

EXTRA! Join or Die

DEAR CHRISTOPHER,

Many of the basic thoughts in your ancestor's diary have made me reexamine my life, both as an immigrant and just as a normal, reflective human being.

Herein, however, lies the second biggest factor—beyond religion and church involvement—which compelled me to revisit Ollis's diary so long after discovering it: his newspaper reading.

As a news consumer since childhood, not to mention having had a long career as a university media instructor, I was and am struck by the diary's frequent allusions to news and how it was presented, consumed, and digested by Ollis during his turn-of-the-20th century years. In our own day, of course, *newspapers* barely exist as physical products in the form of broadsheets and tabloid-journals, but migrating online as they have has given them new life in cyberspace, and news itself is still consumed by readers and viewers who want to know what's going on locally and globally. It's a way of joining our private minds, or what's left of them, to the sprawling public consciousness of the world at large, and we still do it, too much in fact as we have it ceaselessly and ubiquitously on our phones, handhelds, laptops, desktops, and big-screen televisions. It distracts, addicts, informs, provokes, anesthetizes, and tranquilizes in its confining cocoon, holding us captive in all times and places.

Do you think that following big events from beginning to end on CNN or BBC, or in the *New York Times* or *The Times* of London, is new? Not according to Ollis's diary more than a hundred years ago. He does much the same thing with World War 1, the sinking of The Titanic, and other events of emotional impact during his time. The Spanish-American War of 1898, famously sensationalized, even orchestrated, by newspaper titan William Randolph Hearst, is but one example.

On the 16th of February that year, Ollis wrote, "Learnt that the U.S.S Maine blew up last night in Havana Harbor, Cuba. 253 men lost."

March 29: "Congress does not like the President's peaceful policy. Seems to be in for war with Spain."

March 30: "Preparations for war is being pushed with might and main by the government. The President is trying to avoid hostilities if possible."

April 12: "Congress now wrestling with the war question."

April 20: "The President signed the Ultimatum with Spain, giving that power until Saturday to decide what it will do, vacate Cuba, or fight with the United States."

April 22: "The war is now on. The U.S. Gunboat Nashville took a Spanish merchant vessel, and towed it to Key West, Fla."

April 28: "Our war vessels demolished the Forts at Matanzas, Cuba."

December 8: "The Spanish and American Peace Commission at Paris finished its task."

Fittingly, the event was packaged rather neatly beginning with an explosive lead-in, followed by tense, rising action, and closed out in standard melodrama, all of which stated to the reader that something big happened but now it's over, and you can await the next grand event in anticipation of more drama. There will be impact, unusualness, prominent people, each news value intensified by conflict, emotion, proximity, and verbal currency. Folks will be talking about it. You will be one of them.

EXTRA! JOIN OR DIE

Fourteen years later, Ollis peered into the world of newsboys out on local city streets shouting EXTRA! as news of The Titanic spread across the world. On April 15, 1912 he committed the event to his diary, writing,

> The white Star Liner "Titanic" rammed by an ice berg in the North Atlantic Ocean Saturday evening at 10. As I laid my pencil away, the newsboys were shouting EXTRA! out on the street. Getting a copy, it had the terrible caption: "The Titanic foundered, 1347 lives lost!"

Beyond the natural emotion of this news event, the story may have possessed even greater impact for Ollis as the sinking of the great ship occurred near the likely route of his emigration voyage from Norway decades earlier. He may have been thinking that except for timing and God's grace, that could have been the ship he was on, plunging unfortunate souls into the dark, freezing ocean while the ship slipped beneath the surface. It was certainly a justifiable EXTRA! story distributed by the newsboys of his time. And consistent with Titanic's tragic public narrative, the story of newsboys themselves told the equally tragic reality of homeless children, barefooted, recruited by publishers who saw their potential as little merchants and town criers to exploit, sleeping on the very streets and corner alleys where they peddled their broadsheets. They were not the loveable little rascals and street urchins packaged by Hollywood.

So, in all of this, Ollis was a willing participant in his rapidly expanding news culture, for better or worse, a reality which would have surprised exactly no one.

Norwegian-Americans seemed primed for it, in fact, by their own tradition of newspaper reading and publishing, a micro-industry that had begun two decades into their immigration, the 1840s. They looked into the future and saw printed words on newspaper pulp, producing more than five hundred publications, at least four hundred as newspapers, by the 1940s.

The way to join in the spirit of America, they concluded, was to buy into the values of staying aware, knowing where you came from and where you were going, packaged in a common-man (and common-woman) format. A front page might have as many as seven easy-to-read columns of type, fifteen stories, and by Ollis's time at least one dominant photograph allowing everyone to see something as well as to read. Letters from readers, advice for new immigrants, food recipes, folk-remedies and medicines, and down-to-earth stories of Norwegian-American accomplishments, were all parts of the editorial mix. Ministers were often the editors, framing editorial content in acceptable church tradition while minimizing individual quarrels and community dissention, the goal being solidarity whereby the community could speak with a unified voice to an emerging America already compromised by petty polemics and disagreements. Norwegian-American journalism could, at least in theory, educate its readers to come together and agree on positive ways of moral reform, charting a path toward social movements such as temperance societies. Politics were largely Republican and theologically Protestant, endorsing liberty, equality, and patriotism; with Democrats and Catholics held at a distance in the private and public judgment that they brought corruption onto the American political landscape.

The more enduring essence of Norwegian-American newspapers, however, was their effort to stay grounded in four Fs: family, faith, familiarity, and friendship. When they moved away from these values, and when subscriptions and advertising decreased in market-driven America, they could add a fifth F: failure. Where they avoided demise, as with the ever-successful *Decorah-Posten* of northeastern Iowa, which continued into the 1970s before it joined half a dozen other surviving Norwegian-American newspapers, was when they presented themselves to readers as "an encounter with an old friend," according to commentators. Ordinary life was their public narrative, manifested by the reporting of "great and small things from town and country, births and deaths, weather and wind, old ways of livelihood and new enterprises," according to Odd Lovoll. Newspapers provided "a large, clear window" that framed the home community for readers, a community that valued roots, past, and heritage above all else as it melted into the flow of American cultural history. To a high degree, this was about

EXTRA! JOIN OR DIE

having informational security to counter insecure immigrant life. Elisabeth Koren, in fact, said in her diary of *Emigranten*, the standard immigration newspaper for Norwegians, that reading it was the next best thing to receiving personal letters from home.

Here, we might also add that as subsequent generations of Norwegian-Americans gradually became more American and less Norwegian, it is useful to think about their media habits in the larger context of American newspaper history. Ollis, moreover, may well have cut his teeth, so to speak, on the Norwegian-American press, but by the time of his diary seemed much more a viable and committed consumer of news encountered by all Americans regardless of their ethnic heritage. He seemed to have adopted the less-folksy side of American journalism in favor of the more-sensationalized narrative of the large dailies. This was a public consciousness that transcended the ordinary, leaving it behind for the progressive experience of worldwide information and global cognition. His new channels enabling the transformation probably included *The Minneapolis Tribune*, which later merged with *The Minneapolis Daily Star*, or *The Minnesota Pioneer*, which did the same thing with *The Saint Paul Dispatch*. Each paper would easily have been picked up from his front doorstep, or in the case of EXTRA! editions from newsboys working the streets of Saint Paul and Minneapolis.

It is well worth taking a look at the evolution of American newspapers up to Ollis's time in order to better understand his public consciousness—indeed, the public consciousness of all American news consumers in the late 19th and early 20th centuries—and how it came to dominate the lives of so many Americans who loved it, hated it, were indifferent to it, but were encapsulated within its grasp.

It's a dramatic story in itself, Christopher, and how lucky was I to have spent years sharing it with generations of students.

Bear with me.

I used to divide the historical narrative into four parts: newspapers before America, newspapers in early America, key developments and symbols, and the 1830s-1920s. I had a fifth part, too,

The Norwegian's Diary

Christopher, going from the 1920s to the present day, but I'll spare you that story as Ollis's time coincided mainly with part four and marginally with the other parts.

Newspapers, or something like them, go all the way back to ancient Rome and to what was known as the *Acta Diurna*, a government publication that allowed Roman citizens to contribute observations of life in the empire. Not much is known about it other than the fact that it attempted to satisfy a need for public information. In time, papyrus and parchment gave way to early forms of paper, and at least one paper mill is said to have existed in southern Europe. Many centuries forward brought the hugely important invention of moveable type through the efforts of Johannes Gutenberg, who printed the famous Gutenberg Bible in the mid-1400s as well as other publications birthing literacy, audiences, and professional information work in Europe. Then, in the 1600s, a German publication in France, *Relation aller furnemmen und gedenckwurdigen historien* ("Account of all distinguished commemorable news") is thought to have been the first authentic newspaper, a weekly published in Strasbourg.

The first American newspaper, a four-page, two-column publication that included a single blank page for reader response, was known as *Publick Occurences, Both Foreign and Domestick*. It was birthed in 1690 Boston and was shut down after a single issue over its report of cruel prisoner treatment by British colonialists. By 1704, the British themselves were in the game, publishing the government-controlled *Boston News-Letter*, a double-sided, two-column weekly offering news from London and British loyalist news in the American colonies. It was followed by the Franklin newspapers, first the *Boston Gazette* in 1719 by James Franklin, and later by 1721's *New England Courant*, also produced by James until younger brother Benjamin took over following its suppression by the British over material judged as seditious. These were times when press freedom in America was being incubated, and the Franklin legacy of witty, sarcastic commentaries on American life under British rule was being integrated into how Americans would come to think of the press's adversarial role in the country's development. That role still exists, of course, though it has fluctuated in intensity over the years.

The part I referred to as "key developments and symbols" always began with the famous trial of John Peter Zenger, a German immigrant whom in 1734 was acquitted of seditious libel against New York's governor, William Cosby. Zenger defended himself by arguing that what he had written was true, which set the stage for libel defense cases even today. As long as your journalism is verifiably true and not presented maliciously, you'll enjoy First Amendment protection under the United States Constitution.

As you might imagine, Christopher, we then discussed the importance of press freedom, but we often got sidetracked by examining political cartoons of the era, projected on overhead. It was a way of lightening the mood, as I now recall. And the cartoon that evoked the biggest response was the one with the words "JOIN, or DIE" printed beneath a snake broken into eight parts. Each segment of the snake's body represented an American colony or region, with the intended message being one of restoring the snake to wholeness as a plea for solidarity among the colonies. Sometimes we talked about the binary philosophy in America where everything is cast as one thing or another—Republican or Democrat, Protestant or Catholic, liberty or death, black or white, slave or free, etc.—so the "JOIN, or Die" cartoon was a good fit. You, whoever you are, wherever you're from, and whatever you're doing in America, better get with the program or just die. It's that simple. The cartoon was attributed to Benjamin Franklin, whom we discussed at length along with Thomas Jefferson who once wrote that he'd prefer newspapers to a functioning government. His exact statement was, "Were it left to me to decide whether we should have a government without newspapers or newspapers without a government, I should not hesitate to prefer the latter."

We began part four, the 1830s-1920s, usually after a semester break when everyone felt refreshed and ready to continue. Newspapers had become very inexpensive during that time, as cheap as a penny, sometimes two cents, rarely more than five cents, per issue. So, basically everyone in America could afford to indulge in newspaper reading during this *penny-press* era. Horace Greeley, a champion of the time, not only because he made his *New York Tribune* available to all but because he insisted on journalists being ethical and factually accurate, left an important imprint suggesting that if you're going to do journalism in America, do it right. Influential papers such as *The North Star* followed by carrying an anti-slavery torch featuring the famous abolitionist Frederick Douglas and the best African-American contributors of the day. Several times in the diary Ollis himself affirms the anti-prejudice spirit he inherited (which we will later question, by the way), which was no doubt augmented by his newspaper reading.

As we worked our way forward to the 1880s and beyond—Ollis's time—we noted the enormous changes in newspaper publishing wrought by the two competing moguls, Joseph Pulitzer and William Randolph Hearst. Pulitzer arrived on the scene first, employing a combination of sensationalized, crusading journalism which increased circulation of his *New York World* from the low five figures to over half a million in a short time. He did some good things, of course, though he came to be associated with the term, *yellow journalism*, a pejorative for denigrating exaggerated, sensationalized, even fictional reporting for financial profit. His chief rival in their unholy war was Hearst, waging a battle for subscribers that peaked in the late 1890s with Hearst's alleged exploitation of the Spanish-American War. He was said to have invited a graphic artist to "furnish" him with pictures from Cuba, and he would "furnish the war." Hearst vehemently denied this, and no supporting evidence for the statement was ever found. What emerged as true, however, was that the long trail of newspaper journalism, from its foundational moments to Ollis's time, had led to a morally-questionable, profit-making enterprise; an industry inviting, nay pressuring, all Americans to JOIN in the PUBLICK realm of emotion and cognition or perhaps DIE without it.

This was the context of Ollis's newspaper reading, Christopher.

We're all so defined by long cultural histories that precede us, and it's only through coming to know these histories that we can effectively understand who we are and why we do what we do in life.

Just as our lives have been defined by a mix of print and electronic media—mostly by television—so your ancestor Ollis had inherited a public consciousness which at times was noble and righteous, and at other times sensationalistic and ignoble. We don't even know how the younger, digital generations of today are being defined; we have ideas tested through research, of course, but the things we're mostly certain about are that digital natives are socially connected but exhibit many forms of negative behavior, depression, and addiction. But then to say that we were never addicted to radio and tv, or that the earlier generations were not addicted to a newspaper mentality, is to deceive ourselves into thinking that the proverbial old times were so different from the present times. There is a component of American life that has always worked against finding and exercising our better selves, our private contemplative selves, and that component lies buried in media. It was alive a long time ago, and it lives today. We can and do escape it through discipline, meditative cognition, and just living simply like Thoreau, but it has a way of creeping back to reenter our lives and to compromise our better selves yet again. It's a cross we bear.

I should close this chapter, Christopher, with some final thoughts on the loaded word, EXTRA!

It's easy enough to frame the word in newsboy nostalgia, and to add that *EXTRA!-fication*, if you will, was just an earlier version of our *BREAKING NEWS-ification* today. But we can go farther than that.

We can, for instance, realize that printing EXTRA! editions of a newspaper between the normal rhythm of daily editions was a killer of moderate news consumption. Indeed, it was a killer of moderation itself. It was the newspaper industry speaking out of both sides of its mouth, promising genuine psychological rewards from staying aware of important news, while simultaneously taking over your private mind with constant, unending public verbiage. No need to wait for the morning edition to know that something happened somewhere, it seemed to be saying, or that you have to exercise any patience at all before learning something new. Floating the following afterthoughts was its game:

Why wait?

Why be patient?

What are you going to fill the downtime with anyway?

We're the only cognitive opportunity anyone really needs: the public narrative opportunity. We offer the best chance to get out of your private, solitary mind and to JOIN the world of what's happening collectively. We can take you away. And into places of activity. We've got the facts, the information that will make you say wow, the important people, the range of emotions, the conflicts that will make you forget about your own personal conflicts, and the source of all the things you can socialize through spirited conversation with friends and family. We have it all right here in EXTRA!

And EXTRA! can mean different things to different people. It isn't limited to the concept of more. It can mean extraordinary, exciting, fresh, new, inviting. It can be the transformative experience of living the life that you have always wanted.

It can beat the competition.

It can get there first.

It can get you into the game and even be a chip in a bigger game, the proverbial wheel of fortune and winning. You'll be a winner.

So, buy into EXTRA! Take this opportunity to JOIN. And win.

Isn't that what America is about?

As Ollis laid his pencil away on that fateful evening of April 15, 1912, what was he thinking as he rushed out into the streets of Saint Paul with the newsboys shouting EXTRA!? Nothing, perhaps. Or, everything.

I really do wonder.

Lingering Question 7: Is mass media the American villain we never saw coming, and how much can the social divisiveness in

American culture be attributed to the historical merging of information consumption and the profit motive of capitalism?

Short Answer: With market-driven journalism going back at least to the politically-infused subscription battles between Hearst and Pulitzer, it was inevitable that the so-called *social-responsibility* ethic of the American press would be sacrificed on the altar of what we have today: focused micro-marketing aimed directly and only to the exclusive audience that consumes the product. High-minded abstractions such as objectivity, fairness, and balanced news coverage resonate solely when it is our own chosen objectivity, fairness, and balance. In short, the only information that moves the needle, so to speak, in our politics and personal worldviews occurs when we the consumers allow our very specific needle to be moved or not moved. It's not only easy to exclude other values and opinions from the ones we hold onto, it is paramount to maintaining our comfort as humans who like to believe things in a certain way. Give me what I already believe, and I will buy your product, be your friend, and recommend you to others; don't even try to stretch me. Had the press in the *United* States evolved less as a business-driven confirming force, and more as a non-sensational, profit-as-secondary effort, we might well enjoy a healthier American society, both psychologically and practically-speaking.

CHAPTER SEVEN

Contexts of Survival

BEING IMMERSED IN THE daily public world of newspaper reading may have at times seemed a key driving force in Ollis's life, but, somewhat ironically, I do not believe it. More likely is the probability that unfolding a local broadsheet each morning or evening served as a form of light escape from his soul-taxing work life which he spoke often about in the diary. In his rare hours that facilitated longer blocks of time for reflection and contemplation, he seemed more prone to opening books of substance that satisfied his hungry, and private, mind. I observed a similar phenomenon in my immigrant grandfathers, both of whom could be seen reading newspapers, listening to radio, and watching early television, but never as much more than marginal, moderate leisure activities. One grandfather was somewhat of a literary man, often quoting Shakespeare in the course of daily life, while the other was a voracious consumer of fundamentalist Christian literature. Books were more important to them than secular newsprint.

One evening in 1913 Ollis dropped a full bucket of boiling water on his bare feet, scalding them so badly he had to be out of work for a month. As he reflected on this, the most physically painful chapter of his life, he found its silver lining soon after, writing, "I spent most of the time reading." Reading what? A year later during winter 1914, he added, "Finished reading Redpath's 'History of the World.' Was quite an undertaking." Though he had misspelled intellectual historian John Clark *Ridpath*'s surname, his reading of Ridpath's multi-volume global history provided an important clue into Ollis's life motivation: study. Indeed, he may well have held 2 Timothy 2:15 in the forefront of his mind: "Study to show thyself approved unto God, a workman that needeth not to be ashamed, rightly dividing the word of truth" (KJV). Generations of biblically-informed readers have used that verse as the foundation for nurturing a bold life of the mind that resists distractions.

Though common Norwegian-Americans, as documented, seemed to prefer newspapers to books, their penchant for book-reading is also certainly a factor in their history. Iduna Bertel Field's diary, for instance, brims with mentions of book-lovers' catalogs, literature, and literary biographies which she read voraciously. (Just three days after Christmas one year, she wrote disappointingly on December 28th, 1913 that "by to-night I have [already] finished reading all the books we got for Christmas.") In fact, reading books occasionally brought children and adults together into participatory reading societies, whereby the socialized consumption of books offered a kind of prototypical literary fandom for their participants. Topics may well have included romanticized portrayals of Viking lore and other idealized recollections of the Norwegian homeland, and as many as fifty children, women, and men, gathered in indoor or outdoor spaces, celebrated the printed word and the engaging story.

Even more common were book-reading families, whom in the contexts of church and faith, gathered around spiritual literature as a way of augmenting the content of Sunday sermons and other church information sources. Lovoll offers a stunning full-page photograph of a young family intensely focused on two open books. The mother and father appear to be comparing insights while six children listen. Dressed in formal attire, the family seems destined for some kind of faith gathering whose preparation included engaged study. Or, perhaps it was a *family-worship* scene, a common practice among 19th century immigrants from Protestant traditions. Usually a morning activity, family worship began with a reading of devotional literature before progressing toward prayers for a variety of subjects: the church, the country, foreign missionaries, or private individual concerns. Following the prayers, family members dispersed, spiritually energized.

Not all reading was religious, of course. On an individual level, some Norwegian-Americans read books as a form of self-education, which seemed to be Ollis's motive for consuming great books. He, too, quoted frequently from works of classic literature, and he liked to commemorate the birth and death anniversaries of influential figures such as Shakespeare and Scotland's national poet, Robert Burns. Reading was a way of escaping subcultural limitations of language and thought for immigrants, and books existed apart from physical labor, making money, and being compelled to participate in America's prosperity-driven economy. One might have even seen the book as an anti-capitalistic symbol itself, an object that could be savored for standing free from materialistic gain. Not everything had to be a pocketbook or bank account issue; increasing the power of mind was its own reward for the intellectually curious.

Where intellectual curiosity was absent among Norwegian-Americans, reading still prevailed, often as a force that solidified one's place within the subculture. So, it was not always an external driver catapulting readers into the wider world. Rather, it was ofttimes an anchor that kept immigrants from drifting away on the waves of an unknown ocean of strange and unfamiliar experiences. Homeland imagery, the maintenance of memory, and the forever feeling that no matter how well one adapted to life in America, Norway was the real home, the place of true security. The subcultural Norwegian-American literature that grew from this emotional platform was melodramatic, preachy, teachy, excessively moralistic, and far removed from the realistic stories within American literature at large. So, it wasn't taken seriously as literary art, though now more than a hundred years later we have a greater appreciation for adventure, mystery, and romance as subjects that stand on their own, possessing their own value for different, not necessarily inferior, audiences.

Contexts of Survival

And some of it was art even by the rigor of realistic critical standards. Books such as the better-known *Giants in the Earth*, by Norwegian-American author Ole Rolvaag, offered as realistic a portrayal of the immigrant experience as one could find anywhere. It provided readers with a tragic, deterministic vision of Norwegians sojourning west into the Dakota territory against all the crosscurrents one could expect to encounter in such a risky endeavor. A pioneer family in *Giants* . . . is joined by three other families in the quest for land and betterment, but they encounter enough suffering in the process that only immigrant pain remains. Many readers would have been forgiven for desiring a lighter, more romantic tale from Rolvaag, but against the odds of weather, pestilence, loneliness, hunger, and poverty, it is the realism that effectively carries the story.

Strangely, it would seem, Ollis never mentions either Rolvaag, *Giants in the Earth*, or the precedent stories attached to both author and novel in the diary, despite their considerable influence among Norwegian-American immigrants. The easy answer to this is that the book was not published until his final decade of life, and he just never got to it. Also, he was a man of the city, and a rural story might not have resonated with him, even though its painful themes of adapting to life in America would have.

The best reason might be that Ollis had fallen under the spell of history, and the macro view of human events spread across time and place provided the context he desired for the balance of his life.

"Quite an undertaking" [but well worth it], might have expressed his complete thought on that winter night of 1914. Something was deeply satisfying about disciplining himself to follow Ridpath's historical narrative from beginning to end. History is long, deep, and conceptual, providing context for a self-educating individual trying to grasp where he or she might exist amid the flow of world events. Perhaps Ridpath had given him a straight-line view of those events, a more or less logical ordering of things that happened over time. Or, maybe history seemed more like steadily falling dominoes with each tile leveled by the previous tile which then caused the next one to fall. A possible cyclical image of trends and events repeating themselves might have even been Ollis's takeaway. In any case, whatever an ordinary reader received from reading history was not what he or she was going to get from reading melodramatic subcultural literature or the choppy, context-less, fact-by-fact reporting of a daily newspaper. A hungry immigrant mind wanted, indeed craved, more.

In our own day, "Five Reasons Why You Should Read History More Than News," by contemporary blogger Donald Latumahina, suggests that the reader of history will not "get lost in details," will "see the contexts of events," will "read only what is truly important," will "recognize patterns in what's going on around them," and "won't reinvent the wheel" by falsely making one think there is anything new under the sun. History's "collective wisdom," its filtering out of "unimportant stuff," and its "patterns" of recurring events from which one can take appropriate actions to improve life, round out this blogger's perspective.

While it's possible that Ollis entertained similar thoughts a century ago in his post-Ridpath moment, he may well have viewed his reading of history more as something with which to frame his life specifically as an immigrant. History equalizes the past and the present, rendering the past *as* present and the present *as* past in a kind of existential unity by which an immigrant might find comfort. Maybe leaving home wasn't such a great idea, and maybe present circumstances are harder than one anticipated; yet having a retrospective view of what happened while accepting what continues to happen ties both ends of the continuum together in a way that says look, it's just your story, get used to it, and you might learn to enjoy it. Similarly, because world history encompasses a finite world of places, it tends to connect one's old geography with his or her new place of residence. It's only one planet; you used to live on that part of the planet, and now you're over here by means of human migration. Had Ollis been alive today, he might well have encountered Jean Manco's book, *Ancestral Journeys*, which documents the constant movement of homo sapiens having

European origins from one place to another, caught up in the inertia of cause-and-effect human sojourning.

Much more could be added here. History speaks only one language, its own, for instance, lessening the impact of language differences as factors that separate people who need to live together in peace and cooperation. History can also justify religious faith through retrospective stories, even when the stories recall troubling events—the Crusades, the Inquisition, the oppression of nonbelieving minorities in the name of God—showing them to be only parts of an evolution toward better goals of faith and sacramental living. History grounds, stabilizes, theologizes, quiets, and silences, all by showing us that we are part of an ancient, continuing process moving us from the beginnings of our humanness to our current humanness to a future state of who we are, have always been, and will continue to be.

Context context context, the informational backdrop that allows us to make sense of life and the world around us, is ultimately what reading history provides, we might say, whether or not one is an immigrant or someone who has never left home. But what was the specific context provided for Ollis by his reading of Ridpath? What was the possible significance of this particular historian's sprawling *History of the World*?

My best guess begins with the fact that Ridpath was a contemporary voice for Ollis, having been born in 1840, ten years before our diarist. Beyond the natural identification facilitated by being of similar age, moreover, was the fact that Ridpath was very much a self-made person, beginning life poor, receiving a frontier education in what is now rural West Virginia, and reading so prodigiously that he was recruited by a local school to teach at seventeen years old. By nineteen he was in university, then a full professor in his twenties, and shortly after an author of political, geographical, literary, and international histories widely accepted as authoritative by his contemporaries. His three-volume *Cyclopedia of Universal History*, later republished as his eight-volume *History of the World*, was Ollis's chosen text, before it was revised and republished as a massive sixteen-volume set similar to the multi-volume *Story of Civilization* by Will and Ariel Durant in our own time.

Topically, Ridpath's history ranged from "Primeval Man" and "Distribution of the Species," through populations spread across the ancient world; through the Europeans, inclusive of "The Norse Races," and eventually to the newer worlds of Australia and the Americas. Phrases such as "the career of the human race," "the development of social institutions," and "the story of all nations," were packed into the subtitle of Ollis's version. Early reviews of Ridpath's history cast it as within the ability of average readers to understand its content, despite its length. It was presented in plain English with each section being clear, bold, and accurate, requiring neither advanced education nor sophisticated verbal abilities to comprehend. And most importantly, it was packaged as being current and contemporary, which meant being presented in the specific context of Social Darwinism, a prevailing philosophical backdrop at the time of its publication, 1894, and still an active way of seeing world history to and through the World War 1 era when Ollis picked it up.

Social Darwinism, birthed by scholars in the 1870s, sought to apply Charles Darwin's biological "survival of the fittest" concept to societies and economies in which only the strong experience progress while the weak gradually diminish until nature eventually excludes them. It was virtually dead by World War II when it became linked to Naziism, eugenics, and scientific racism, but before that time it possessed wide appeal even among religious seekers of the day who tried to see God's ordering hand in the underlying determinism of life's events. Ollis, whom as previously mentioned, seemed Calvinistic in his belief that God was life's sovereign influence even if the ultimate purposes of the supreme being weren't readily known, would have been attracted to Ridpath for that reason alone. Reading a history of the world that articulated a sense of human destiny dictated by external forces consistent with that Calvinistic faith was persuasive. Being compelled by promise or necessity to leave Norway, then finding himself caught up in uncontrollable and inescapable trappings of American life, would have had anyone acknowledging those external forces, whether they had been imposed by nature or by God. Harsh yet strangely comforting in its truth, this was the context provided by Ridpath for an honest man seeking stability amid his poverty, his difficult work life, his social challenges, and his family tragedies.

So, he read, and he read, and he read some more. "Was quite an undertaking," he emphasized.

I think again of my immigrant grandfathers, whom like Ollis needed to contextualize their lives as a means of surviving their own particular circumstances. I identified most with my maternal grandfather, who seemed to prefer classic literature as his context, yet I knew my paternal grandfather better, as he lived well into my adulthood. He had a tiny bedroom library full of religious tracts and books by John R. Rice, a leading Christian fundamentalist in his day. Rice's newspaper, *Sword of the Lord*, was also there promoting an uninspiring gospel of old white men in gray suits, awkwardly limited and judgmental even to a boy. I wanted no part of it myself, but I saw how essential it was to my grandfather. It grounded him in certainty, secured like an anchored boat on a choppy, restless sea of an insecure existence. That choppy sea was his life and world as an American immigrant, and though I never understood the waves that tossed him about, I could see something very real in his instinct to survive. It was the same instinctive image that arises from Ollis's diary.

Lingering Question 8: Will the anti-status-quo nature of book reading continue to evolve as the one single virtue ensuring the survival of the American mind in future contexts and environments?

Short Answer: The challenges to reading books, and reading them right, would seem to be immense in today's world. Finding the time to read books might be first among the obstacles, but that is nothing new when we consider, for instance, that reading time was always limited among generations trying to survive work and life commitments. The greater challenge, *right-reading*, consists of a loss in the ability to experience the true nature of meditation and contemplation that frames the linear communication of books. Even when new generations find time to read, the spiritual cognition gained from a pre-digitized existence seldom exists unless substitute cognitive factors are available to facilitate a right-reading mentality. Reading well requires reflection on the intake of logical, linear stimuli, without which there is little human capacity to imagine or even to experience the sense of spatial memory existing in prolonged reading. Some things might be gained: the capacity to assimilate bytes of information with greater speed than ever thought possible, for instance, but such communicative experiences lend themselves more to uniformity and dependency than to an ability to transcend status-quo enslavement and have an independent mind. Spilling superheated water on one's feet might give you some time off, but what you can do in and with that time may be an unhealthy mystery.

CHAPTER EIGHT

Clinging to the Myth of a Departed Captain

A FEW MORE THOUGHTS about contexts: they are, at best, imperfect; at worst, dangerous.

They're subject to the rightness, wrongness, or calculus of problematic approaches to the possibility of truth on the part of providers, a subject best deferred to insightful epistemologists, from the ancient Chinese and Greek philosophers to the wisest contemporary voices.

And they're something we choose, more often than not based on what we already believe and want to believe and what we think we know from personal experience. Confirmation is our game because there is comfort in feeling confirmed by contexts that make us feel as though we're on the right road to all of life's meaningful abstractions, especially knowledge, wisdom, and ultimate truth.

Racism in the late 19th and early 20th centuries, the subject of this chapter, can be, and was, contextualized through media (newspaper reading in Ollis's day), social and natural sciences, theology, or as with Ollis, history. Reliable history was a reasonable context, though as mentioned Ridpath's history was steeped in Social Darwinism, a questionable means of understanding race because it exploited the theory of evolution to show, scientifically

The Norwegian's Diary

no less, that some races were inherently weak and inferior and therefore subject to stronger, superior races, played out across human history. It could have been worse, of course, as with my grandfather's fundamentalist context and his following of the all-confirming white supremacist theology of his day, which inched him along in how he felt and perhaps wanted to feel about God, race, and the superiority of being a white man.

But let us return to Ollis's diary to draw some of these ideas together.

It is clear from the diary that Ollis was never completely removed from white racial conceit during all his years of committing pencil to paper. On December 19, 1912, for instance, he wrote, "At my shipyard, it is always too cool for a white man to work." Then, on October 11, 1916, he added, "I detest that work. It is not for white men, and I will not stand for it very long either." Many similar comments were set down from the 1890s-1920s, some more troubling than others, such as Ollis's perspective on the relocation of his church from urban Saint Paul to a suburban outer ring that was becoming popular among white residents eager to separate themselves racially.

> A meeting was held at our church—to vote if we should sell our church at 13th and Broadway. The vote was carried by a big majority. Most of our people have moved into the Midway district [and] would like to shorten their distance to the church. We can buy a neat little church out there for a reasonable price. Another reason is that the district around our church is fast filling up with Africans. (October 11, 1921)

Nothing excuses or justifies such destructive, racially-charged conceit, and indeed I witnessed similar behaviors in my immigrant grandfathers. Each fled the inner city along with their churches, commonly basing their *white fright* on inertia produced by the mass exodus of security-seeking friends and neighbors wanting safe spaces for their loved ones. Civic crime was the overt rationale often stated by this escape-minded class, but below the surface a less-spoken mentality of *us versus them* churned and percolated.

CLINGING TO THE MYTH OF A DEPARTED CAPTAIN

I am sure that my ancestors would have preferred *us and them* as their defining emphasis, but *versus* was certainly part of the racial equation. Let *them* remain in their black civic spaces where *they* belong; *our* place is away, elsewhere, removed, and with our own people. Racial exclusion is a many-layered beast.

In truth, though, I do not think they, or indeed Ollis himself, wanted to be that way. It was just easier. And there was another side to it that involved reaching out from one's place of security in an effort to reduce or even minimize the reality of racial separation. My dear grandfathers genuinely came to see their local inner-city communities as mission fields, places and people to serve through the lay ministries of their now-suburban churches. They wanted to go there, be involved, do some good; and back at home, if one listened closely, one could hear that racism existed mainly on the surface, not in the depths. Occasionally, a hero from another race would emerge from the worlds of culture or life, projecting an image illuminating the fact that a common humanity existed. Making an effort to acknowledge this truth was something to nurture, not fear.

As harsh as Ollis's racial diary entries were, moreover, there were plenty of others that revealed a proverbial *other* side.

On March 8, 1898, for instance, he wrote, "They do say that slavery is abolished in this country, but I am inclined to doubt it." A year later while trying to empathize with the black, turn-of-the-century experience in America, he couldn't seem to wrap his mind around "what a black man saw in a white man's country" (August 12, 1899). And in the closing weeks of the century, he wrote on December 6, 1899 that the "papers brought accounts of a most diabolical, fiendish and revolting lynching of a Negro at Mayville, Kentucky." He was referring to the lynching of Richard Coleman, a 19-year-old black man who had confessed to killing his white boss's wife but was never given a trial in a court of law. Finally, there were moments in the years ahead when Ollis seemed to gather glimpses of race-based hope as on July 4, 1913 when, while reflecting on the American Civil War, fought over slavery, he expressed his hope that "the animosity [of those days] is, at last dead and buried, and that the whole of our great and glorious country is . . . united into one people, one nation, happy in the assurance that such a conflict will not again disrupt it."

He would occasionally go back on that hope in challenging moments of personal doubt and suffering until the diary ultimately fell silent in the 1920s. Along the way, he seemed to reflect the sense of racial confusion that periodically diminished, then resurfaced, in constant repetition, a uniquely American civic rhythm incorporating partisan political messaging, inconsistent theologies and philosophies, interchurch battles, crises of false and misled conscience, and many other obstacles that prevented coming clean in a country that could never quite achieve peace between the races. Indeed, America was an obstacle course for immigrants of conscience who viewed true, moral satisfaction as the goal of the contest, and who placed the heart above the head, the heart above what one had been taught, the heart willing to perish like Huckleberry Finn who opted for going to hell in order to facilitate the freedom of slave Jim.

In churches, the "reemergence of the issue of slavery" periodically raised its lingering divisive wand among Baptists, Methodists, and Presbyterians throughout the years of Ollis's diary, more so in the 1800s than after, but it was a problem that had a long shelf life, according to *Denominations and Denominationalism: An American Morphology*. "Backing away from [racial equality] standards for church membership and ordination" of clergy was also an occurrence. Public proclamations celebrating black freedom and rights were seldom popular in conservative white churches, so to avoid divisive acts and messaging such ideas rarely surfaced in congregational discourse. Norwegian-Americans, of course, tended toward the more accommodating Lutheran churches, and with the exception of the always-conservative Lutheran Church Missouri Synod, racial attitudes seemed more progressive.

Norwegian-Americans, however, had other obstacles to hurdle. *Nordicism*, the racist ideology holding that the Nordic race was both superior and threatened, was a subtle form of conceit present below the surface of even the most well-intentioned

CLINGING TO THE MYTH OF A DEPARTED CAPTAIN

immigrants. In *The Viking Heart: How Scandinavians Conquered the World*, Arthur Herman offered that it was as old and deep as the texts of ancient mythology, writing, "Aryan excellence seemed to find its purest expression in Norse religion and myth... a vigor of imagination shown nowhere by men of non-Aryan blood." Herman added the painful truth that "Norsemen became suppliers catering to the insatiable appetite for slaves across the civilized world." My father-in-law was fond of saying that there were two kinds of people in the world: Norwegians and those who wish they were. This was said mostly tongue-in-cheek by a good man, but the statement belied an underlying superiority not unlike forms of conceit applied to Anglo-Saxons, Franks, Aryans, and other white populations hailing from northern Europe. Any levity in such comments, however, tends to disappear whenever destructive, horrifying racism resurfaces, such as in the 2011 massacre of children and adults in Norway by Anders Behring Breivik, who car-bombed downtown Oslo before executing dozens of children at a summer youth camp. According to his manifesto, Breivik's Nordicism was directed toward Islamic immigrants and those who facilitated their integration into Norwegian life.

A more widespread obstacle to morally positive racial clarity among Norwegian-Americans involved the simple desire to fit in. Most saw slavery and overt public racism as "abominations," according to Odd Lovoll. But "adjusting to the society in which they lived" produced a need to "conform to the ways" of that society even if it meant sacrificing higher ideals. It would have been easier to have stayed in Norway where a clearer path to moral positions and conclusions on such matters existed and where one could participate more freely in progressive movements toward societal betterment. In America, that path was muddied and sometimes washed out completely despite the best intentions of the morally-minded populace. Too many obstacles, and in labor-intensive American society, too little time.

Then, there was the obstacle of bad theology, which for lay theologians and lay church leaders like Ollis, imposed a shaky foundation for, and an unclear channel to, definitive truths about slavery and race. Biblically, the instability emerged from misapplying Genesis 9:25 to people of African descent: "And Noah said, cursed be Canaan; a servant of servants shall he be unto his brethren" (KJV). The story of what became known as the Curse of Ham emanated from a moment or period of drunkenness by Noah and the observation of his nakedness by his second son, Ham. Noah's other sons, Shem and Japeth, had been told of this by Ham but chose to cover Noah's body to conceal his naked state. When Noah awoke and discovered what Ham had done, he cursed him with a fate of servanthood, saying his legacy would be as "a servant of servants," which over time became attached to slavery, black Africans, and the history of black enslavement.

There were obvious flaws, however, in this racist interpretation. The curse was only a man's action, not endorsed by God, and Genesis 9 never said that Ham or his descendants were black. So, these conclusions had to have been imposed by ideological forces to justify black slaveholding, even to the extent of seeing an entire race of humans being cursed *black* by their sins. Of the many books written on the subject, one that readily comes to mind is *Noah's Curse: The Biblical Justification of American Slavery*, by Stephen R. Haynes. While teaching at a southern college in Tennessee, Haynes discovered that the institution had been founded in the 19th century by a confirmed slavery advocate who believed in the Curse of Ham. Research then led Haynes to explore the legacy of the curse, concluding that it had become conflated in America with the basic human desires of *honor* and *order*. "Nothing was more important than honor"; honor "entered the very texture of upbringing"; "southern culture of honor flourished in the ... 19th century"; Genesis 9 would forever be interpreted "in honor-bound fashion," Haynes came to understand. Slavery advocates saw themselves as honorable "patriarchs in the tradition of Noah," he added, and as embodying "the protective authority of a loving father over the entire household of whites and blacks."

But, the misperceived virtue of honor had to be accompanied by the misconstrued structuring agency of order, Haynes implied. Being "a defender of law, order, and property" was the root of "the link between order and African servitude," he wrote. God had meticulously structured his world of natural, ordered processes, and black African slaves were seen as disordered and in need of imposed structuring. At any age they were like children who required forced discipline to counter their half-savage nature that resisted placement in a protective hierarchy, slaveholders managed to persuade themselves. And after Abraham Lincoln's Emancipation Proclamation of 1862–3, when many freed slaves ventured north, these same slaveholders lived to compare the ensuing social chaos of the north with the genteel mannerism which had existed in southern, slaveholding communities. Abolitionists had been infidels, facilitating a sinful society opposing all that God and nature had ordained. It was destructive and certainly worth going to a bloody war over.

How Lincoln managed to balance the rival forces of everything sacred to one society with the rival forces of everything morally right in another society still seems impossible to fathom fully even today. This fact was never lost on American immigrants of conscience, and Ollis, like many, returned to celebrating Lincoln's legacy whenever despairing moments threatened to extinguish hope. One standard way of doing this was Ollis's seemingly required commemoration offered every 12th of February:

> February 12, 1918: (Lincoln's birthday) One hundred nine years ago today this great man was born in a log cabin in Kentucky. No more need be said. We all know him and we all love him. Today even the sun done its best to honour him.

The anniversary of Lincoln's birth, his humble beginnings, his greatness, his fame and appreciation, his honor, his perceived place as a friend of even the milky-winter Minnesota sun, were annual reminders that the sixteenth president had accomplished the impossible, in Ollis's mind. By preserving the union of disagreeable states acting on opposing notions of honor and moral rightness, he did what couldn't be done, and an average immigrant of hoped-for moral resolve which facilitated their own survival as an American citizen wasn't going to forget it. Even if the tributes repeated the same themes, they were very much sacramental like a recited Eucharistic rite performed regularly in places of worship.

Lincoln had always been an immigrant's president, starting with his birthing and nurturing of The Homestead Act of 1862 which opened up free land, invited foreigners to emigrate, and showed them that America would be hospitable to the arrival of new social groups and ethnicities. The *Act* fixed welcome, possibility, opportunity, and the promise of government for and by the people, into the psyche of both arrivals and pre-arrivals. And there were biographical, indeed *mythological*, virtues attached to the man which had spread across the print landscape once Lincoln had become famous; virtues especially meaningful to curious immigrants like Ollis. Lincoln's early life as a hungry reader, for instance, of everything from the King James Bible to John Bunyan's *Pilgrim's Progress, Aesop's Fables* to William Scott's *Lessons in Education*, Shakespeare to Lord Byron to Robert Burns, mythically crafted an image of the humble man from Kentucky and Illinois as the seeker immigrants could become or at least emulate in the context of their own humble circumstances. Also, for ones such as Ollis, the image of Lincoln as a person of survival-driven faith and service, and a man who had a Maker, not ashamed or afraid to acknowledge and consult a higher power when things seemed hopeless, resounded each time a birthday or anniversary was referenced.

In *Team of Rivals: The Political Genius of Abraham Lincoln*, Doris Kearns Goodwin concluded her massive history by reflecting on Lincoln's mythic reach throughout the world of potential emigrants, like the rural Russian horseman who "trembled" at the mere sight of Lincoln's image carried to a tribal chief. That incident, according to author Leo Tolstoy, proved "how largely . . . Lincoln was worshipped throughout the world." His "peculiar moral power," Tolstoy added, "was bigger than his country—bigger than all the [American] presidents put together." The mention of Lincoln's name, his supremacy, his transcendent image which became larger than the land that bore him, had catapulted him into a stratosphere beyond that of mortal men, not for himself but for all. That was and still is his legacy.

Without elaborating, Kearns Goodwin also references American poet Walt Whitman who is almost always part of the conversation about Lincoln's legacy. Just as Lincoln was the American immigrant's president, Whitman can be appreciated as the immigrant's poet. While hoping without reward that Ollis would make some mention of Whitman in his diary, I reread my worn, 1882 *Leaves of Grass* volume and was reminded of how immigrant-friendly were the images throughout Whitman's verse. He spent generous amounts of time speaking of "destiny," the "puzzle" of the New World, the "busy, teeming, intricate whirl" of America, and the cities and towns of "mechanics," "carpenters," "masons," "boatmen," "deck hands," "shoemakers," "wood cutters," "mothers," "young wives," "the girl sewing"—all in an endless cataloging of immigrant laborers who were invited to the party. "Come, I will make the continent indissoluble," he wrote. "I will make divine magnetic lands . . . I will plant companionship thick as trees along the rivers of America . . . along the shores . . . the great lakes . . . inseparable cities."

And, of course, there were the four poems linked directly to Lincoln and his assassination on April 15, 1865: *O Captain! My Captain!* (1865), *When Lilacs Last in the Dooryard Bloom'd* (1865), *Hush'd Be The Camps To-day* (1865), and *The Dust Was Once The Man* (1871). The three latter poems drew together the images of "sea winds blown from east and west" (*Dooryard*), "life's stormy conflicts" (*Camps*), and "the foulest crime in history" (*Dust*) through a seamless merging of both metaphor and reality which harbored the perfectly-bonded image of Lincoln in the pathos of *the* lost American icon. However, it was the *captain* metaphor in *O Captain! My Captain!* that became the classic image familiar even to children who read the poem, or had it read to them, in school. The captain who freed the slaves, said we were all equal regardless of skin color, and warned that our house would collapse if we didn't learn to accommodate each other's differences, was "fallen cold and dead."

Many Whitman scholars and commentators see *O Captain! My Captain!* as one of the poet's least brilliant poems. Too traditional, too simplistic, and inferior to Whitman's free-verse masterpieces, as it has been judged over the course of a hundred-fifty-plus years. From an American immigrant's point of view, however, Whitman's enlistment of the captain metaphor could not have been more persuasive. Immigrants arrived in America by ship, placing their trust in their captains' skill not only to navigate treacherous seas but to establish and maintain harmony, peace, and the hope of safe arrival during the voyage. Passengers had a dream of reaching a distant, unfamiliar port, after which they might move on to the ultimate prize of a new life offering fulfilled opportunities they had been told about and now risked everything to realize. They depended in large part on the captain to get them there. Wrote Whitman: "O Captain! My Captain! our fearful trip is done/The ship has weathered every rack, the prize we sought is won/The port is near, the bells I hear, the people all exulting/While follow eyes the steady keel, the vessel grim and daring . . . ."

This was the myth worth clinging to in Ollis's eyes; the myth that justified an immigrant's hope that America could transcend its flaws, its sins of racism and division, even if its heroic captain had departed in an episode of tragic violence.

Hope may well have been the immigrant's only true friend.

Lingering Question 9: Will America ever have another Lincoln, and even if it does will it be able to recognize him (or her) and have the necessary humility and moral fortitude to break through its now-instinctive prejudicial mindset which disallows human differences?

Short Answer: Among the many themes existing within the enormous Lincoln canon, a most prominent one is that, without a Lincoln, America is unable on its own to establish a permanent form of equal justice for all and the moral accommodation of others. Divided, it wallows and wobbles, threatening to collapse at any moment and take the world with it. Even more concerning is the practical reality that any sort of normal, balanced individual will never be able to garner enough political support to carry a majority vote, much less appeal to elites in Congress and the courts. One can easily argue that fandom and personality cults will rule America's political future, and that the winners of elections will be the ones who have the most fans. One can even argue that a fandom template was set a long time ago, beginning perhaps with Lincoln himself, whom as a witty, storytelling, homegrown common man, who looked good in the visual media of his day, tilted the scales enough in his favor to capture the public's imagination and thereby win the day. Fan cult leaders, however, rarely have such universal support, and so the future would seem to continue in its likely trajectory toward fragmentation and division.

CHAPTER NINE

Labor and Lament

DESPITE HIS OCCASIONAL LITERARY references in the diary, Ollis never mentioned Walt Whitman. The poet's Lincoln poems were apparently not a strong enough reason for a moment of commemoration, and it is certainly possible that Ollis had never read them. It is also likely that a man of the church such as Ollis, who may have been at least marginally aware of Whitman's ambiguous sexual reputation, would have avoided him on that basis alone. We'll never know any of this, of course, so all guesses here are exactly that: pure conjectures.

Indeed, one additional speculative thought is that even if Ollis had come across an edition of *Leaves of Grass* at some point, Whitman's optimistic portrayals of the American workforce would have been seen as naïve. All those rosy references to mechanics and carpenters, shoemakers and woodcutters, working happily in pre-labor-union America would have struck an unhappy laborer like Ollis as unacceptably inaccurate. The problem would only have been compounded if a reader of Whitman came to know something of Whitman's own unhappy work life, which began at age eleven and included stints as an office boy, an apprentice, a printer's devil, a typesetter, compositor, pressman, distributor, home deliverer, low-level laborer of odd jobs, victim of economic downturns such as the Panic of 1837, failed school teacher, and ineffective journalist, not to mention being called out publicly for being a *sodomite*, which likely limited new job opportunities to few or none. These factors would have been headscratchers for readers seeking authentic portrayals of working Americans rather than romantic images of them by someone who knew better.

Ollis's work life, moreover, was anything but romanticized poetry. Swallowed up in laissez-faire capitalism's industrial world of hard labor, he was hired, fired, spat upon, laughed at, dumped on, insulted, and physically worn down beyond his seventieth birthday when his limbs and appendages finally gave out and the diary went quiet. The laborious lives of my immigrant grandfathers told a similar story of workplace oppression, one grandfather being regularly ridiculed for his Polish-Ukrainian accent and his inability to understand bosses and coworkers, the other actually dying from lung cancer produced by his year-in, year-out breathing of second-hand tobacco smoke. The caveat, of course, was that they almost never talked about their work lives, so as family members we had to assemble their realities from puzzle pieces sporadically articulated in conversation. To this day, I know only that my language-challenged grandfather was a machinist in the bowels of a Detroit foundry, and that my lung-cancer grandfather worked in plumbing. Going to work each day was like going to war for them, which was the other topic men of that day rarely talked about.

Perhaps Ollis was just as tight-lipped in face-to-face conversation. Confiding in the quiet recesses of the diary, however, gave him a way to vent emotional pain from humiliation sufficient to produce physical illness, interpersonal miscommunication sufficient to produce hatred for those in authority, overwork sufficient to produce feelings of dying, oppression sufficient to produce robotic apathy, job insecurity sufficient to produce loss of consciousness, and unending physical torture sufficient to produce an absence of hope. Any month of any year told the story:

> March 16, 1898. I was not at all satisfied with the outcome of the shipping clerk controversy. I therefore went to the manager and told him he would have to decide whose duty it was to write out my orders. And just like

the knave and despot that he is, he would not do so, but simply ordered me to do it as heretofore, despite my protestations of being overloaded already. He also made the ridiculous remark that I had more leisure than any other man in the House. Never before in my life have I felt so overwhelmingly humiliated and disgusted. I was actually sick all the rest of the day. Oh, how hard it is to be a poor man, sometimes.

March 27, 1899. Orders terrible. I am working myself to death, if I don't get some sort of relief very soon.

April 9, 1900. The only thing that sustained me during this awful day, was that I preserved a stolid indifference as to how the work went. I did not care in the least about any possible results.

October 3, 1916. And now comes a sorry tale. As I came down in the basement, leaving for home, I was handed a letter which, when reading it at home, informed me that I was discharged for lack of work. I nearly fainted.

September 14, 1920. Terrible hot day, and to add to it I was ordered [at seventy years old] to work in the lumber yard piling hardwood lumber. The broiling hot sun was certainly awful. This was one of the hardest days in all my life.

Such was the "sorry tale" of this Norwegian-American's life of labor and lament, in his own futile words. Rather than growing into any profession, or evolving with any company or enterprise, work was never celebrated as the thing that occupied time in such a way that justified the necessity of earning a living. It was only something to tolerate: a means to an end, accompanied by an awareness that those at the top knew they could exploit the suffering and survival of those beneath them. Thus, the well-known Nordic proverbs that *hard work never killed anyone,* and *hard work equaled the worship of God,* tended to melt under the burning reality of immigrant labor in America.

Labor and Lament

Lovoll wrote that "life in the great cities of America was difficult," and that work "in the mills and factories" was best expressed by one word: "toil." Arduous toil was a hard and continuous balancing of weariness and pain often with no clear end in sight. Fortunately for Lovoll's beloved Norwegian-American community, barely a quarter lived in cities at the turn of the 20th century. Whereas the other three quarters chose farming, fishing, logging, and other land-and-sea based professions, the less fortunate quarter struggled in an urban world for which they were never really prepared. Outdoor workers could also struggle mightily, but at least their historical familiarity with the mainly rural environment of *mother* Norway had them better acquainted with agrarian life. Urbanization, on the other hand, did not come naturally, forcing proverbial square pegs into round holes which made fitting in, interpersonal communication, and following the instructions of bosses and "despots," in Ollis's words, more challenging.

Knowing from the diary that Ollis's brother Charles had continued west to the Pacific coast, I wondered constantly if Ollis had considered following him and whether his immigrant life would have been easier, at least in the context of work. Nothing more is said about Charles's life, though, and Ollis gave no serious indication that he ever thought of leaving Minnesota. The Twin Cities of Minneapolis and Saint Paul had become the urban capital of Norwegian America by that time, and judging by some of Ollis's cultural interests, he found that part of urban life engaging, even appealing. His affinity for church life, too, was an anchor that might not have existed out west where formal religion, especially the Lutheran faith, was less of a factor. Churches were fewer in number and influence in and around Charles's Seattle where a more outdoor life was prized, and where the practice of outdoor rituals in the natural world seemed more important to West-coast residents than the indoor rituals of Midwestern faith communities. So, Ollis stayed where he could be a lay minister among others of his race, albeit paying a steep price by having to labor in adverse urban conditions.

The Norwegian's Diary

He appeared to work in some type of intense clerical capacity possibly at one of the local sawmills that produced lumber processed daily from Minnesota's sprawling hardwood forests. Indeed, the 1880s of Ollis's immigration arrival were referred to by some as "the decade of sawmilling and lumbering," according to David C. Mauk in *The Heart of the Heartland: Norwegian American Community in the Twin Cities*. It was a decade, and a profession, even "more labor intensive" than that in other industries, before and after," Mauk adds. So, Ollis's complaints about being overloaded with orders, likely originating with builders in Twin Cities home construction, were constant, and persons of Norwegian background may well have preferred being out in the woods sawing and cutting rather than stuck behind a desk piled with invoices. Backbreaking outdoor labor was no doubt excruciating, but it might have been preferred to mind-numbing indoor work, and in choosing the indoor option, as Ollis seemed to do, his ethnic soul was taxed to an unsustainable degree. Further, as the diary mentioned, if orders were slow, he was expected even as a senior citizen to break his back stacking lumber out in the yard. All of it was accompanied by the hovering presence of task masters hired to make sure there was no drop-off in productivity, and that even the subsistence wages paid out to a laborer like Ollis were accounted for by profit-minded managers and owners looking to advance their interests.

It should also be said that by Ollis's time as an immigrant, the 1880s and after, class solidarity among laborers was visibly emergent. Scandinavian-Americans, moreover, were often instrumental in furthering the argument that America was in dire need of a fairer balance between employers and the employed. Rights, the sharing of production, better pay, more reasonable work conditions, safety on the job, more adequate training for the operation of heavy machinery, and ultimately surviving potentially destructive free market forces, were in the labor conversation even before Ollis's time. But they were slow to be implemented, and Ollis was never on the receiving end. Furthermore, even though his fellow Norwegians, Danes, Swedes, and Finns were out front in labor reform, those who had ascended to high positions of ownership and oversight could be just as oppressive as *despots* from other ethnic groups. That "knave" who had ignored Ollis's plea for help in late winter 1898 might well have been from his own Norwegian-American tribe.

This *system* could corrupt anyone, even his own people, he may have been thinking. It lacked a soul, and those caught within its grasp could end up just as soul-less, character-challenged, and bitter throughout the balance of their trouble-filled lives. "Where is the golden land, where are the golden people?" an immigrant quoted by Mark Wyman offered. "What has happened to human feeling in such a great wide world . . . a land [supposedly] flowing with milk and honey?" Plain and simple, it would have been healthier to stay in Norway, on the open spaces of one's youth, where one might be poor but at peace in the long retreating shadow of his Viking heritage. You took the emigrant's risk, however, and now had to let it play out, not at all as you had dreamed but rather as reality had ordained it. In the increasing disquietude of your sadness, you had no choice but to own it. We all have to live with the choices we make.

Wyman's *Round-Trip to America: The Immigrants Return to Europe, 1880–1930* clearly elucidates the fact that it was the labor problem in America which, more than anything, caused immigrants to retrace their steps and return home. This was part of the "splintering" effect of life under "industrial capitalism," adds Gjerde and Qualey in *Norwegians in Minnesota*. Not ironically, the fifty-year period of Wyman's research was exactly two years short of Ollis's immigrant timespan, 1880 to his death in 1928. Upon further elaboration of this perilous half-century, Wyman isolates several problems that were significant enough to have Europeans forsaking their American dreams and admitting that the annoyances of where they came from were not as bad as the problems they encountered in the United States. If giving up the dream for the place you first dreamed it brought peace back into your life, then it was a sacrifice worth making.

Many questions surfaced.

The Norwegian's Diary

Why, for instance, should any person have to live with the anxiety produced by being forced to do more than what was reasonable in one's work? Nearly everything, from executing complicated production strategies to operating sophisticated machines, was handed off to workers who were seldom adequately trained for the work. Yet, they had to do it to avoid receiving the kind of dismissal and reassignment notices that had nearly caused Ollis to faint where he stood. Henry Ford himself had over ninety percent of his unskilled foundry workers doing such jobs which he said even "the most stupid man can learn in two days." Wyman also points out that employers blamed immigrant employees for being both dumb and ignorant if the subtleties of English could not be effectively decoded when instruction was offered. Ollis was obviously fluent in English, as illustrated by the diary, but detailed fluency was simply out of reach for many immigrants, like my Polish-speaking grandfather whom to his dying day had never mastered fine points of the English language.

Why, also, were needed periods of rest so hard to come by during the workday? Under the constant gaze of roving foremen, for instance, anyone caught stopping to rest was either removed after a harsh warning or, like Ollis, accused of enjoying undeserved and excessive "leisure." "A Norwegian," Wyman quoted, "got a job digging ditches in Duluth, Minnesota, in a crew of nine watched over by a man with a cane. If anyone took a break, he was there at once threatening him and warning him that he would be thrown out if he didn't work." This triad of warnings, accusations, and threats of dismissal formed the laborer's daily emotional backdrop, not surprisingly evoking responses such as Ollis's lament: "Oh, how hard it is to be a poor man, sometimes."

It was hard, too hard. And as Wyman suggested, many immigrants were their own worst enemies, tempted by a "money now" factor that caused them to accept brutal jobs rather than turning to the slower payouts of agriculture and other slow-yielding outdoor work. Again, regarding brother Charles, Ollis may have chosen not to go west with him because urban employment in Saint Paul offered a quick financial fix. He would do the work, however awful, to receive the money which allowed him to marry and start a family in the progressing social environment of the Twin Cities. His life fulfillment would have to come from that matrix, building his dreams as a man of family and faith and not from the satisfaction of having a rewarding career. Immigrants who chose that option for their lives often enjoyed the richness of bringing children into a world of family picnics, civic celebrations, excursions, fatherly and motherly nurture, and watching their children grow up strong and healthy. But no matter how well domestic life played out for them, the tortures of their employment dragged them down into a despair that never went away regardless of how happy homelife made them.

As a practical reality, it is possible that the only immigrant class from Europe that was truly able to cope with the dark urban labor experience in America was the class that saw the work was temporary. These were the ones, according to Wyman, Lovoll, and others, who had contingency plans upon arrival. They crossed the Atlantic in the short-term mindset of a temporary worker who could take advantage of American industrial growth accompanied by definite plans to return home carrying as much money, and perhaps material goods, as their transit trunks could hold. It was always a risk, of course, because the future was uncertain, yet many did accomplish a profitable remigration experience, going back home prepared to restart their lives where they had taken their first breaths.

Despite his dreamy remembrances of his "dear old" pre-1880s Norway, the diary offers no evidence that remigration for Ollis was ever a real possibility. It had to have crossed his mind, however, on days when work threatened to destroy him. If so, it would likely have crossed his mind accompanied by a number of asked and answered questions: *Was he too old to go back?* He was already thirty in 1880, and fifty in 1900 when the despairing work thoughts increasingly trickled from him like drops from a leaking faucet. *Were his roots sunk in too deep?* His church depended on the continuation of his participation and lay leadership. *What about his family?* His children were already second-generation American citizens with no known desire of being uprooted from friends and local activities. *Would life actually be better in Norway for a fifty-year-old common clerical laborer who had been away from that country's own rapidly changing ways for decades?* Near to the time when the approaching insecurities of World War I threatened everyone in Europe, remigrating would not have been a secure option for any immigrant's return. *Would his financial situation have allowed an expensive transition to occur?* Precisely, no, as he repeatedly complained in the diary about having little extra money for anything, let alone a transatlantic move.

As an intelligent and well-read layman, Ollis may have even concluded like novelist Thomas Wolfe a few years later that, *You Can't Go Home Again,* so why even dream about it? In personal letters from remigrants who had returned to Norway, it was clear that they often were not welcomed back with the open, embracing arms they had expected. The stories they told of life in America, for instance, were sometimes seen as *Amerikaskroner*: exaggerated adventures that inflated the egos of storytellers self-promoting themselves and their experiences among home bodies who had stayed behind. Of course, if the remigrants brought back cash that could be converted and then invested in Norwegian businesses or in land purchases, the reception was more favorable. Then, people at home could see that the immigration risk had paid off, and returning home to do something constructive gave the remigrant a justifiable social status. Coming home empty-handed with only stories to tell, conversely, labeled one a failure unworthy of much notice.

That would have been Ollis's situation as a potential remigrant. So, he did the only thing he could have done: persevered for the rest of his life in American immigrant survival mode as "a poor man" trapped in the amber of his day, exactly as his diary now preserves him. And as with thousands, perhaps millions, of other immigrants in his time, unrewarded by the dream-inspired risks they had taken, a gradual disquietude set in. They stood firm in a state of noiseless anxiety, an uneasiness manifested in reduced talking and writing, and a drop-off in allowing opportunities for others to peer into what was happening internally within their souls, souls well captured by Henry David Thoreau's enduring comment: "The mass of men lead lives of quiet desperation." Thoreau added that a "stereotyped but unconscious despair is concealed even under what are called the games and amusements of mankind. There is no play in them, for this comes after work."

After work. No play. Unconscious, concealed despair. And the *disquietude* of an ageing man that probably had his grandchildren asking, *Why is Grandpa always so quiet?* seemed very much to define Ollis's final years as expressed in decreasing volume by the diary.

He had not yet gone silent, but he was getting there.

Lingering Question 10: Was the famous "quiet desperation" life verdict articulated by Thoreau reflective of an increasing sentiment that for Americans caught within the country's emerging, soul-crushing industrial economy, free will was at best an open question and more likely a troubling myth?

Short Answer: Fortunately for Thoreau, he was able to escape into the woods or on liberating rivers and walking paths, so those quietly desperate men to whom he referred probably were looked at from a distance and not part of his own personal story. Hanging out with his mentor, Ralph Waldo Emerson, in relatively peaceful, semi-rural Concord, Massachusetts, the two transcendentalists in a community of likeminded folk may have frequently mused over others who were never able to *transcend* the industrial clutches that held other men down. At least that is the story with which we are familiar. The real common individuals who labored in hell, so to speak, experienced the tortures first-hand. They were the quiet ones, often immigrants, who had their souls crushed, unable to do anything about the chasms into which they had fallen. It was top-down all the way to the bottom. How the Ollis Evensons of that world would have wished to have had a few moments to enjoy studying nature out at pristine Walden Pond. The destiny they knew, however, did not allow it. They had their families, their churches, their lives and times of holidays and picnics, but in the long run they found themselves thrust back into the work yard, the factory, the smoke-filled office. Is that what they chose for themselves, or had they been only teetering dominos in a line of other falling tiles? It must have seemed that way to a great many of them. The reality we know is the reality we live, and ultimately that is what produces our personal philosophy. Even if we know that wiser people may tell a different story, our own experience rules, and it is always with us.

CHAPTER TEN

Disquietude into Silence

Dear Christopher,

As we move through the final years of your ancestor's diary, I can't help but see it as Ollis's personal record of a disquieted mind slowly evolving into a silent one. Again, of course, this is only his diary, and as he lived another five years after jotting down his final words, he may have chosen to communicate verbally in other ways. Perhaps, too, he may have fallen victim to the limitations of advanced age, with failing eyesight, fingers unable to steady a writing utensil, cognitive difficulties, or any number of problems capable of limiting his ability to keep the diary going.

Then again, perhaps the diary offered a clear, detailed portrait of those final years and the events leading to them, and the disquietude-into-silence essence reflected increasingly from about 1918 to the end articulated the true nature of his final years.

Disquietude, as I understand the word and as *Merriam-Webster* defines it, is "an uneasy state of mind usually over the possibility of anticipated misfortune or trouble." It has a history of usage dating at least to the 1600s, and its synonyms include terms such as *anxiety, uncertainty, tension, distress, hand-wringing, doubt*, and many others. I'll add that hints of disquietude whisper beneath the surface of Ollis's thoughts from the beginning of the diary to the end, though they are often offset by the verbal stability of his faith and the articulation of happy moments juxtaposed with anxious ones. I'll also admit that disquietude is by no means immigration-exclusive, though I have to say that I hear it often from fellow immigrants—including myself, of course—as we navigate our various passages from familiarity to uncertainty. Romanticizing the past doesn't help, either, when it runs up against obstacles to peace of mind and wondering where in the world we belong. Doubt presses in during those moments, and I at least deal with it by telling myself that "on balance" I prefer the life I have chosen over the one I left behind.

We're all different, though, and Ollis's growing sense of disquietude, which began with his normal immigrant responses to uncertainty, climaxed in the double-sided calamity of unchosen, unanticipated circumstances. Side one was about the unending torture of his work life; side two involved family tragedy that chipped away at his stable faith, never crippling it but leaving him nevertheless disquieted.

No one would have blamed him.

Of his seven children, he buried five, and he grievously watched his wife, Hellen Andrea, die at 54 on November 29, 1910. Before Hellen's death, he had buried his institutionalized father, Even, on September 17, 1900, and his mother, Sofia, on March 12, 1903. On November 6, 1897, when nearly everyone was still alive, he nonetheless came home from a hard day at work and, in an eerie foreshadowing of things to come, found his entire family almost dead from sulfur gas that had "penetrated the whole house," he wrote. He watched as each family member was treated for gas inhalation, all surviving the near-catastrophe, "thanks be to God," he added. Then, there were the children: five sons—Halfdan, William Bertrand, William Baldwin, Henry, and Roy, four who died in close succession prior to 1900, the last one, Roy, dying in 1918; and two daughters, Florence and Lillian, who happily outlived Ollis, surviving well into the 20th century, according to ancestry records.

Roy's death is particularly worthy of mention because it revealed Ollis's increasingly disquieted self, anxious and uncertain in tragedy's grasp yet unaccompanied by bitterness of any kind.

Disquietude into Silence

On October 29, 1918 Ollis received a telephone call notifying him that Roy was dangerously ill with pneumonia. The next day, Roy seemed to recover somewhat, and by the 31st he was holding steady. On November 1, however, he suddenly deteriorated, dying early in the evening, with Ollis mustering the strength to commit the event to his diary in the most objective, emotionless way possible: "Roy Stanley Evenson, my last son, died at 7:55 P.M. with pneumonia. He was 26 years, 1 month, and 1 day of age. He was my 5th and last son."

The next day, November 2, Ollis wrote that he could not go to work. The following day he wrote that he could not go to church, and that he might never recover from this event. Emotion had begun to condition his thoughts, threatening even to overrule his otherwise cognitive responses, as he wrote,

> (Sunday) Did not feel inclined to attend church services. I feel terribly downhearted over the loss of my dear boy. I know it will take a long time before I will ever be like my former self. If I ever will.

The final day of the tragic sequence saw Ollis tearfully packing up Roy's belongings and beseeching God to spare his two daughters, writing,

> November 4, 1918: So—it is all over. My last son is laid in his last resting place, which is very near to that of his mother whom we laid there 8 years ago. I am glad that it is over and that we had a very fine day for it. Now, I hope and pray that my two girls will be spared for me. God grant it!

Indeed, his girls were spared, Lillian living an abbreviated life until her death at 51 on January 16, 1937, and Florence enjoying a fuller existence until passing away at 84 on February 11, 1974. Both daughters gave birth to Ollis's grandchildren, who eventually produced greatgrandchildren and spread from coast to coast in America as third- and fourth-generation Norwegian Americans. He would have rejoiced heartily at this generational continuity, though sadly he never saw any of it come to pass, unless in the wake of his own death in 1928 he was able to peer through an afterlife veil from the other side of a transfigured existence.

On this side of that veil, while he still lived, the days, months, and years following Roy's death would have seemed an appropriate time for a searching man's personal *theodicy*: in short, a time for asking and answering theological questions about why, under a watchful God's eyes, we suffer unjustifiably in the earthly state. Exploring *the problem of pain*, or *when bad things happen to good people*, however, were *theodical* ideas still decades into the future, and perhaps the Ollis Evensons of that *pre-theodical* world instinctively knew somehow that asking questions such as *where is God when it hurts*? were always the wrong questions, steeped as they were in overfocusing on oneself rather than simply accepting what happens in life and then moving on. Ollis, despite pleading with God to spare his surviving daughters for himself, never once in the diary asked the question, *why me*? He never asked, why anything? He merely accepted, focused outwardly after brief interior sentiments, tarried over external events, and moved on. Rightly or wrongly, this was the course he and perhaps legions of others whose tendency to accept their fate was built on doubts about the nature of free will, took shape, even after tragedy struck.

How did this play out?

For Ollis, his grief process of November 1918 forced him out of himself and propelled him toward the largest external event of his time; the event that contained everyone else's story of pain, loss, and insecurity; the event that made private, individual suffering seem small and insignificant when compared to what was happening in the wider world: the closing days of World War I. Even before the contours of his personal grief were knowable, he had risen above Roy's death to concern himself in the diary with European nations declaring their independence, allied armies pushing back their enemies, victories in occupied France, British advances and German defeats, and President Woodrow Wilson's armistice negotiations, all occurring within the seven days following Roy's passing. By the actual signing of the WWI Armistice on November 11, ending the war, Ollis was again enveloped within his faith, linking the war's end to the Almighty's oversight of what happens, then and forever. He wrote,

> November 11, 1918: This day as God willed it, is destined in the world's history to be probably the most important this old globe has ever witnessed, save the death of Christ on the Golgotha cross. The ending of the World War took place today. Thanks be to Almighty God!

Christopher, this curious ability our ancestors possessed to detach themselves from personal circumstances, all in the spirit of acceptance and the outward recognition of external things, seems difficult to comprehend in our own day. We seem trapped by our subjectivity, always having to find *the answer* to why things happen and then to send our best guesses out into the world. Sometime around the year 2000 a friend gave me a big green hardback of *Theodicy: An Annotated Bibliography*, by religious studies scholar, Barry Whitney, and I was stunned by the sheer number of books seeking unknowable answers to the problem of evil in the world. And Whitney's two-inch-thick volume included only sources published between the 1960s and 1990s. Exploring evil had become an industry during those thirty years, and though I too love to internalize the questions faith in God raises, I couldn't help but wonder if the old way, Ollis's way, my grandfathers' way, of accepting and moving on, was healthier. We're so good at complicating things. Jesus never says go home and read a lot of ponderous books before deciding to follow him. He simply says—like a *Nike* ad—*just do it.*

As with Ollis's projection of his grief onto the World War I backdrop, a point of curiosity in my own family history once emerged from something similar. My maternal grandfather, who suffered from lung cancer caused by breathing in second-hand smoke, died immediately after the assassination of American President John F. Kennedy on November 22, 1963. As a family, we internalized our grief for a moment but then moved on from it as details of the JFK story came under the public spotlight. The televised funeral, the grieving multitudes, the swearing in of President Lyndon B. Johnson alongside a stunned and suffering Jackie Kennedy covered in her husband's blood, the live shooting of assassin

The Norwegian's Diary

Lee Harvey Oswald by Dallas club owner Jack Ruby, were so dramatic and impactful, we as a family never really had a chance to obsess over the death of our beloved grandfather. We could have seen this as a case of inescapable distraction, facilitated by media, but all these years later I like to think of it as the necessary projection of our own grief onto a vivid awareness of a world suffering its own unimaginable horror. It was no time to be overfocused on ourselves, and no time to think of ourselves as alone in our private human drama. There would be time for that, but it wasn't at that instant. No one would have understood this better than the Norwegian American immigrant whose diary said so much about his grief in so few words.

In any case, Ollis's disquietude after Roy's death seemed to be gradually replaced by an increasing fall-off of things to talk about in the diary. He could have said much more about the WWI aftermath, as so many immigrant sources have said for over a century how importantly the War acted as a threshold for immigrants finally and definitely subscribing to the American ideals of power and prosperity; a marked contrast to an unstable Europe suffocating in old smoldering ruins and uneasy politics of its pre-World War II existence. There were a few more work complaints, though, and mentions of the bicycling knockdowns on the streets of Saint Paul, but the final three years of the diary offered mostly tepid, stoical comments about local news events, church activities, and the weather. On the verge of going silent, the diary reminded me of the final pages of Jon Krakauer's book, *Into the Wild*, which I had read just before visiting the Como Lake estate sale, in which the young man, Christopher McCandless, ended his own diary with the words, "beautiful blueberries," before starving to death in the Alaskan hinterland. Ingesting toxic potato seeds had brought about his rapid demise, whereas for Ollis the decline was more a gradual silencing that seemed to say, "I'm so tired, and the time for expressing myself through written words is over."

Silence.

Even more than the topic of theodicy, the literature exploring silence is a vast universe of subject matter encompassing the whole of epistemological experience. Think of any academic discipline, attach the word *silence* to it, and you get the picture. It is philosophical, historical, theological, and literary; an essential feature of social and natural science; a definitional and utilitarian subject focusing on uses, abuses, types, ranges, structures, processes, subtleties, dangers, and annoyances, neither confined nor contained by any existential narrative or cultural approach. Silence can be a bad thing or a good thing; a goal of living for the stoic philosopher, Epictetus; something potentially more valuable than speech for the spiritual master, Pythagorus; a universal refuge for Thoreau; and a friend that never betrays, according to Confucius. For our common-man immigrant, Ollis Evenson, his diary's ultimate silence could have touched upon any of these concepts, though knowing him only from his private, personal thoughts expressed through pencil on paper, we have to risk the conclusion that his ceasing of words as a record of his existence was very likely a form of spiritual silence borne from resignation and the more important act of listening in spiritual silence to his Maker. One recalls the like-minded Nordic immigrant, Iduna Bertel Field, and her poetic images of silence as "God's answer," God's "deep unspoken Word," and the fact that "silent I am one with Thee."

Another book that mysteriously appeared in my life of sharing and receiving great books with readers I have known was the novel, *Silence*, by the Japanese writer Shusaku Endo (*Endo Shusaku*, to the Japanese). It was given to me by a Japanese friend sometime before our trip to Japan decades ago, and I was never sure why. Perhaps it was to show me why it is so difficult, or impossible, for the Japanese to accept western Christianity, or the Christian religion at all. Or, maybe it was simply because the book offered a compelling fictional narrative of clashing cultures during the time of European expansion into the Asian world of the 16th century. The Portuguese, who were the first to sail their ships to India, Macau, and ultimately Japan, primarily for trade reasons, also had evangelistic motives at each destination. And in Japan they were successful for a time until Japan's leaders grew suspicious, then fearful, believing that their culture and native religious

The Norwegian's Diary

beliefs were being uprooted by the intrusive, uninvited Christians. Torturous, murderous persecution of Japanese converts followed, soon accompanied by acts of forced public apostasy in which Christians risked death if they refused to step on a *fumie*, an image of Christ, in renunciation of their faith. The evangelizing priests were also forced to apostatize by knowing that in failing to do so, their followers would be tortured and killed in their stead; so rather than being able to undergo their much-preferred martyrdom for staying true to their faith, they too stepped on the fumie, thereafter going completely silent. No preaching, no evangelizing, no discipling, and importantly no living as a European while they remained in Japan. Silence, and living as a Japanese serving only Japan, was effectively their destination and the end of their voice.

Critical interpretations of *Silence* have traditionally explored the evident theological depths of Endo's great book. Nuanced symbolic essays focusing on God's silent companionship with his followers during adversity have been counterbalanced by critiques exploring a more indifferent, inattentive God who is insensitive to human suffering. Symbols of silence abound, with the sea being the most prominent one: an unspeaking carrier of humans voyaging to precarious fates and destinies, a silent giver and taker of life, an indifferent swallower of drowning humans, a silent place of persecution and punishment; all interpretations leading back to portrayals of the silent God, best expressed by the book's main character, Father Rodrigues, who says rather fatalistically, "... like the sea God was silent." Other interpretations have reduced the impact of theological themes in favor of playing up the book more as a specimen of historical fiction narrating the story of Japan's "hidden Christians" (*Kakure Kirishitan*), who seem to emerge in the final pages of *Silence*. The priests have apostatized, publicly rejecting all discernible traces of their past, but the Christian faith continues secretly in Japan, enduring exactly as one might expect: in silence.

Over the fifty-plus years since its publication in 1966, I have never seen an interpretation that sees *Silence* as an immigrant story, a failed one at that. But the basic topical ingredients would seem to allow such a reading. The apostate priests sailed from Europe with many dreams: the dream of spiritual adventure on the high seas, the dream of fulfilling their calling as servants of God, the dream of harvesting lost souls who might find their reborn selves in relationship with Christ, and the dream of a fulfilled personal destiny. The fact that such dreams didn't always come true, at least not in the ways one expected, is precisely what happened to legions of immigrants crossing oceans of anticipation in the hope that their stories would end as happy ones. These immigrants were often anonymous heroes, "the simple little ones in society," according to Einar Haugen, a Norwegian American linguist. Poor in funds and often in spirit, but with hopes for a better life, they crossed the ocean with a few belongings that might have included a Bible, a hymnal, or anything else that secured them spiritually in their barely imagined destinations. Lacking in formal learning or even basic communication skills, they worked where they could find work and lived where life seemed possible. Lucky ones survived America's grinding gears of industry and social chaos, holding fast to an after-hours life of spiritual exercise and intellectual enquiry.

And some, like Ollis Evenson, kept diaries, before the diaries themselves fell silent—as silent as slowly descending snow, blanketing their world in obscurity until someone, anyone, at some future unknown time, allowed them to speak again.

The year 1923 seemed as good a year as any to have a diary fall silent.

It was an in-between time. The *war to end all wars* was now buried five years in the past, and despite Germany's bitter defeat, other nations celebrated even in their anxiety and uncertainty as their daughters and sons returned home, many bearing battle scars, but at least bearing them away from the muddy, impersonal battlefield trenches of the war.

The next big global event, the Great Depression, was still six years in the future, and few were anticipating a stock market collapse or the even bigger event of the following decade: the onset of World War II. This relatively peaceful interval of time, moreover, offered economic prosperity to many who were employed in the *right* industries: automobile production, aviation, film, radio, and the smaller enterprises that served them through product development and technological innovation. Cultural progressiveness, too, was evident in music and fashion, art and literature, architecture and design, all nurturing attitudes of novelty and variation such as improvisational jazz, expat literature prioritizing practicality over flowery prose and poetry, and descriptive, era-defining movements such as art deco. Advertising, magazine publishing, celebrity endorsements, sports fandom, science fiction, and ubiquitous forms of entertainment all were thriving in 1923 and beyond. It was, after all, *The Roaring Twenties*, a decade that did roar for many but not for everyone.

In Ollis's Minnesota, the local farming economy whimpered while other industries roared. Exports of farm products which thrived during the war suddenly dropped like a stone as revenues were cut in half, forcing many off their land and into city life where they could earn a living. Ollis, of course, was already a city dweller, and there was nothing in his diary to suggest that he didn't benefit at least marginally from the economic prosperity of the lumber industry, or wherever he was employed during his final years. The poor man of the diary, however, may have remained poor to the end, which also could have been a reason for going silent.

A more likely cause of the silence for a righteous, pious man like Ollis was a widespread recognition in America that, despite the post-war prosperity and feverish cultural activity, the world was emphatically not a better place. Racial violence, battles over the teaching of science and religion in schools, threats of communist infiltration, prohibition and those who subverted the law to profit from it, were on the increase. Indeed, squeaky-clean Saint Paul fell prey to gangsters eager to corrupt the local police establishment, bribing their way to the concealment of their nefarious underground marketing of alcohol across the country. Then, there was the fact that in America everyone seemed to be talking: on telephones, in industry, on the street, in culture where even the famous silent films of the era were disappearing in favor of the first *talkies*: movies that synchronized spoken words with images. Life was changing so rapidly, so dramatically, why even try to keep up with it in a slow-talking diary by a man, now in his seventies, living in a nearly empty house replete with memories of deceased family members and unrealized dreams? Silence was a better alternative.

Most unfortunately, we don't know if any of this was true, but one does like to speculate on what caused Ollis to go silent.

For me, after twenty-five years of contemplating the diary and the man who wrote it, I imagine him enjoying a quiet evening in 1923, sitting in a comfortable living room chair, open Bible on lap, dreaming of his eventual entry into his New Jerusalem above.

For His name's sake.

Lingering Question 11: Is *acceptance* and the *silence* that accompanies it evidence of the once-unthinkable proposition that we as human beings don't really have free will, or are they merely a final expression of the helplessness we feel in a world where problems seem too big to solve?

Short Answer: Despite some current scientific literature favoring the *no-free-will* opinion (*Determined: A Science of Life without Free Will*, by Robert Sapolsky, 2023), *the expression-of-helplessness* opinion seems more likely, at least anecdotally. Reducing the question to the anecdotal nature of immigrant diaries, for instance, offers compelling narrative evidence that begins with freedom-of-choice decision making, but ends with human beings overwhelmed by circumstances beyond their control. Expanding such narrative evidence, in turn, and extending it into the much larger sphere of existential reality, seems a reasonable course, too, as we consider the helplessness many feel in a world of unavoidable artificial intelligence, unmanaged climate change, unstoppable nations of power overtaking weaker ones, and other resurfacing ills impossible to ignore. Put the question to Ukrainians and Gazans, at this moment in time, and hear what they have to say. Those would be public thoughts, however, even in person-to-person exchanges, making the private thoughts of personal diaries all the more valuable for their unedited veracity. What do we really say, privately to ourselves, when no one is watching or listening? Are we honest about our doubts? Do our deepest feelings tell a story we wouldn't want anyone else to know? Who are we, really, at the end of the day, when work or play have ended and the last lights grow dim; or at the beginning of the day when we peer into a near or distant future of obligations and living requirements? Those are questions we all have to ask and answer as the passing of time is managed and navigated.

Epilogue
Fragments of a Finder's Diary

Question: How does one end a story about an immigrant's diary?

Answer: With excerpts from another immigrant's diary, of course; in this case, my own. A hundred years have passed since Ollis's "message in a bottle" was sealed, but as Gjerde and Qualey remind us in Norwegians in Minnesota, a century means little in historical context. We may even get closer to appreciating the mystery of immigrant experiences when we juxtapose current fragments of thought and experience with those from the past. Immigration is not a science of certainty, but rather a cause for wonder.

Sunday October 1, 2023
Saint Paul, Minnesota, USA

Walked around Como Lake trying without success to remember the house where I found Ollis Evenson's diary. Hardly anyone around despite pleasant fall weather: mildly overcast, no rain, no wind, no people, that old damned-in-paradise quality I remember well. Manicured neighborhoods and postcard streets, and lonely as a desert.

Drove to the intersection of Raymond and University Aves where Ollis was knocked off his penny farthing. Antique buildings refurbished as lofts, a liquor store, and the Minnesota School of Bartending. Light rail going east and west. Not much happening here, either, but that's just Saint Paul.

Coffee with Megge. She mentioned Mindekirken Gudstjeneste, a Norwegian church her grandmother used to talk about. I attended today's English-language service. High-church Lutheran. Short chat with the minister, Gunnar Kristiansen. Few in the service. How long can traditional churches be held together by pockets of aging parishioners before everything goes extinct? Leif Eriksson festival this week in the adjoining Norway Center. I may return for one or two events.

Tuesday October 3
Saint Paul

Political chaos in Washington. House of Representatives voted to remove the Speaker. No plans for a replacement. In New York, former president on trial for inflating his wealth to get illegal bank loans to prop up his brand. More trials to follow for alleged crimes committed while he was in office.

Wednesday October 4
Saint Paul

Visited the Bloomington Historical Society, housed in a vintage town hall. Respectable small museum similar to the single-topic ones in Europe. Strongest exhibit: a corner of a room devoted to the US-Dakota War of 1862. Thirty-five days, also known as Little Crow's War in which starving Sioux warriors killed hundreds of settlers who were on their land, resulting in the Dakota Sioux being exiled to reservations throughout the region. Thirty-eight subsequently hanged, and the State of Minnesota acquired and sold all Sioux land within state borders. Hard not to feel for victims of genocide.

Epilogue

Night, attended a concert by *Tidlos*, a six-piece Norwegian band whose mission is to preserve ancient hymns through mod-Celtic music. Reminded me of *The Chieftains* from Ireland. Part of the Ericksson festival.

Thursday October 5
Saint Paul

Enjoying all the US junk food, though stomach, joints, skin, and probably my heart and brain, not so much. Spent most of the day at the Minnesota Historical Society—fine exhibits but too much so, spread across three floors with elaborate historical narration and reconstructed artifacts. History gets lost in the production. Less is more.

Saturday October 7
Saint Paul

"Poetry Café" with Megge at the Norway House. Three local poets and two Scandinavian folkies on vintage stringed instruments. No detectable theme other than Nordics and rural life. One poem on Ukraine by poet Sharon Chmielarz seemed out of place, though current after yesterday's attack by Russia that killed civilians in that ongoing war.

Israel under attack in worst military conflict there since 1973. Surprise attack by Hamas with murders and rapes of Israeli civilians and others taken hostage in Gaza. Here we go.

Tuesday October 10
Saint Paul

Informative visit with a volunteer worker from the Minnesota Historical Society. She knows a lot about Norwegian-American history, having studied under Odd Lovoll at St. Olaf down in

Northfield. Lovoll now in advanced age but still lectures occasionally, she said. Invited her and her husband to Lisbon.

Thursday October 12
Saint Paul

Drove through heavy rain down to Decorah, Iowa, two hours south of Saint Paul. Surely one of the most important Norwegian-American centers anywhere. Most of the day at The Vesterheim, a museum campus loaded with artifacts and resources. Good exhibit on the Atlantic crossings with testimonials from those who lived to tell their stories of immense suffering during the journey and their immigrant challenges in the US. Good God, the courage, risk, and insecurity. Picked up two more diaries in the bookshop, one from the 19th century, another from the early 20th. I'll be flying back to Lisbon with a small library.

Saturday October 14
Saint Paul

As a final event this visit, attended a lecture on Hans Christian Andersen at the Danish American Center in Minneapolis. Well-attended. Theme: *Is happiness possible, according to Andersen?* Mixed responses from the lecturer and audience.

Sunday October 15
Saint Paul

Had planned to visit a Lutheran Church pastored by Jason, who visited my church in Lisbon a few months ago, but was feeling sick. Bad eating caught up with me. Drank water all day and felt better by evening. Wrote an apology for missing the service. Packed my suitcases for tomorrow morning.

***

Epilogue

Friday December 1
In-flight to Oslo, Norway

Time for our annual anniversary trip, this year to Norway for a week, paying for most of it with stored-up travel credits. My year to choose the destination, so here we are on the flight to Oslo. Neither of us know what to expect, never having been there. I liked Denmark and Finland, but Marisa has no Scandinavian experience and would probably rather stay in the south this time of year. In fact, I was a little surprised at her interest when I floated the Norway idea. The Viking history intrigues her, as most Portuguese know that Viking ships showed up on the Lisbon waterfront a thousand-plus years ago. They made a few coastal raids in the 800s before moving on to Spain for an invasion of Seville. As always for us, it's more about history than anything else, so this will be mainly a museum trip, I expect, with some local culture, probably.

Saturday/Sunday December 2/3
Oslo

Cold. Dark. Expensive. 1,160 krone (approx. 100 euros) from Oslo Airport to our millennial/gen-z hotel/apartment. Everything, from the elevator to the door activated and controlled through the phone app, as if travel wasn't stressful enough already. Took an hour to understand how to work the interior lights. Picked up groceries at a nearby store; another K1,100. Many things to do in Oslo, so we've decided not to leave the city. A day trip to Bergen would be equal to $1,000 for each of us. Over budget and no way.

Monday December 4
Oslo

Internet facts about Oslo: inhabited since at least the last Ice Age; important haven for the Vikings; officially founded in 1049 CE; once-important 12th century churches now in ruins; became the Captial of Norway in 1299; hit hard by the Black Plague in the

The Norwegian's Diary

1300s; catastrophic fire destroyed the city in the early 1600s, later rebuilt from nothing by King Christian IV of Denmark who named it Kristiania after himself; changed its name to Oslo in 1925 after Norway became independent in 1905. Ollis referred to the city as "Christiania" in the diary. Oslo also occupied by Germany during WWII, and resisters were executed at Akershus Fortress, which we visited in bitter cold. Well below zero, Celsius, with wind: nasty combination for my Portuguese wife who has never experienced cold like this.

Tuesday December 5
Oslo

Nobel Peace Center today while Marisa stayed in the hotel feeling unwell. Wanted to stay with her, but she insisted I explore the Center and report back. Yes and no to all the profiles: Yes to Jimmy Carter, Mother Teresa of Calcutta, and Desmond Tutu. No to Henry Kissinger and Menachim Begin. And a big what?? to Yoko Ono, whose words and images formed a special exhibit. Never realized she was such a contemplative, though. Compelling quotes: "Put your shadows together until they become one," and "Light a match and watch until it goes out." Also, "War is over if you want it." What would John say?

Wednesday December 6
Oslo

Weather a few degrees warmer today, with snow. We managed to walk over to the National Museum, where works by Edvard Munch are on display—including *The Scream*, familiar to most people. Paintings by Gaugin, Van Gogh, and Cezanne also scattered throughout the galleries. Stopped for coffee in a shop with huge windows looking toward the harbor, steam rising from the water. Best painting of all, Marisa said, feeling much better today, thank God.

Epilogue

Thursday December 7
Oslo

Three more museums today: *Maritime, Fram,* and *Kon Tiki.* All excellent. Probably most enjoyed the Fram with its authentic 19th century explorers' ship. Museum goers can walk through all decks, and even though it's not an immigrant ship, we could see berths, living quarters, toilets, the galley for meal prep, a library and various work and activity rooms. The Maritime "Museet" had an entire floor devoted to Viking travel, and the Kon Tiki Museet offered informative commentary on Thor Heyerdahl's famous expedition proving that ancient rafts could have carried South Americans to Polynesia. He was David, of course, challenging Goliath in arguing that some Polynesians hailed from the East, not from Austronesian lands to the West. His genetic data was flawed, though, so traditional anthropologists destroyed his arguments for the most part. Heyerdahl never gave up and, if nothing else, added to what was known about wind and ocean currents. Great exhibit on Easter Island, too. Those strange stone heads never lose their mystery.

Friday December 8
Oslo

Walked through a steady snowfall to a digital, interactive program on the Vikings. Didn't think we would like it very much but were surprised. Even a virtual reality theatre of a battle, with flaming arrows, combatants chopped up by long axes, and a simulation of our own deaths at the hands of a vicious Viking thug. Visually provocative. What was most interesting content-wise was the portrayal of Vikings who had adopted Christianity, often left out of the story, but not here. "It was a time of transition, with ancient pagan culture gradually giving way to a new Christian worldview," according to one wall inscription. Good Chinese restaurant, "The Golden Mountain," next door.

The Norwegian's Diary

Saturday December 9
Road to Oslo Airport

Heavy, blinding snow on the way to the airport. It was sticking to the pine trees along the mostly-empty highway in near-total whiteout. Deep snow outside the airport, making it hard to roll our bags. Haven't seen snow like that since Minnesota days. It made an appropriate ending to a story of a Norwegian immigrant who left one wintery climate for another, one world for another, and a possible reminder that wherever one goes in life, it may not be all that different from where one has been.

***

Thursday February 1
Lisbon, Portugal

Finally healed, I believe, from a stomach virus picked up in Norway. Marisa had it first but felt better after a couple of weeks. More like a month for me. We thought it might be Covid, but the tests for both of us came back negative. Feverish on the TAP flight, Oslo to Lisbon, then mild gastro symptoms through the holidays and into January. Seemed to hang on longer than normal as I'm usually well after a few days. Pretty much back to normal now.

Sunday February 4
Lisbon

Sent an email to the visiting minister at our church, saying we'd be away this week and next. After a hectic week, we just wanted to stay home today, and next week we'll be in Sesimbra for Carnival activities. Long-planned weekend. Feels like I'm heading into one of my dry periods concerning church attendance. I miss the hymns and prayers, but both of us seem to get tired of everything else, especially the after-service fellowship.

Epilogue

Wednesday February 7
Lisbon

Living for daily morning walks again by the river. Nothing is more spiritual. I can totally identify with Darwin, who was said to walk through the countryside while his family attended church. I really wonder if their experiences were so different. Observing nature in solitude seems more than capable of competing with hymns and prayers. My fellowship today was with the birds and feral cats I have come to know, and it's always lovely to see the Portuguese out at low tide filling baskets with shellfish they will sell to the local restaurants. A scene with ancient origins, no doubt.

Thursday February 8
Lisbon

Rain and wind today. Effects of an Atlantic storm named *Karlotta*. Wind ended just before noon, and now steady rain. Love to listen to it and glad I finished sawing up the two trees in the yard that fell during the last storm. The logs now under a shelter to dry out during the no-rain season and ready for the fireplace next winter. Two or three of them will heat the whole downstairs.

Friday February 9
Lisbon

Today is the weekly Romani/Gypsy outdoor market. The Romani continue to be hugely unpopular throughout the country, but everyone enjoys the market. Brings out the medina instinct. Organic produce, wild honey, spices and peppers, clothing stalls, leather goods brought up from Africa, and many immigrants from the former colonies of Cape Verde, Sao Tome, Angola, Mozambique. Women carrying baskets on their heads. Tasty bifanas and frangos grelhados if you don't mind the long wait to be served.

The Norwegian's Diary

Saturday February 10
Lisbon

Carnival started yesterday and will be in full swing tomorrow. We'll be in Sesimbra for it. Reserved a hotel room above the parade route.

Sunday February 11
Sesimbra

One of our favorite places in the world. So simple and ancient. Fishing village where the boats haul in their daily catch and the fishers spread full nets on the beach. What isn't sold goes to the big fish market behind the restaurants. No reason to eat anything but fresh fish here. It's cooked so well with simple spices and olive oil and served with new potatoes, carrots, green beans, salads. Fresh bread and extra virgin always on the table. Lots of Sagres and Superbock, and super affordable vinho tinto, branco and verde. The Portuguese know how to live, a natural set of talents I never really acquired in America. Tips the balance for me, personally.

Monday February 12
Sesimbra

Yesterday, Super Bowl Sunday in the States. Apparently, it was a great game that went into overtime. With me lacking interest as I have so often in the past, and Marisa not knowing much about American sports, we spent the day in Carnival events. Today was the annual clown parade, a big local hit. Thousands of people from all age groups dressed in clown costumes, which we joined in by wearing locally made clown hats. Marisa's resembled a leprechaun's bonnet in bright clownish colors. Mine was more like the tall stovepipe worn by the Cat in the Hat from the children's book series. Celebrations continued all night.

Epilogue

Tuesday February 14
Lisbon

Valentines Day. Fatima, my dermatologist, had scheduled an appointment months ago to monitor my continuing basal cell carcinoma skin marks, giving me a clean bill of health. Afterwards, lunch before visiting the Lisbon Oceanarium for the first time. New Age music, oceanic graphics, and the big aquarium teeming with sea life. The sea otters stole the show, playing and primping as if they knew they were the stars.

Friday February 16
Lisbon

News. Another stateside mass shooting, this time at the rally celebrating Kansas City's victory in the Super Bowl. Many injured, one killed. Prosecutor in the case against the former president, for trying to steal the Georgia state election in 2020, is on trial herself for alleged improper relationship with another lawyer in the case. Stolen documents case also in the works, as is the indictment of the former president for inciting the insurrection in Washington DC on January 6, 2021. Still another indictment for illegally paying "hush money" to a porn star and a *Playboy* model cleared to begin soon. American economy healthy with lower unemployment, lower inflation, and a booming stock market.

Saturday February 17
Lisbon

Shockwaves across Europe after the former US president's new threats to weaken NATO, and the death of Russian reformer Alexei Navalny in a Siberian prison. Putin's signature is on it, according to most news accounts.

Sunday February 18
Lisbon

Energy-less service in church, but with the early Spring weather our walk by the river was today's sacramental treat. Seventy Fahrenheit with a refreshing breeze all the way to the boat terminal. Lovely.

Monday February 19
Lisbon

Heavy Atlantic fog and twenty degrees cooler today. Good day for reading.

Wednesday February 21
Lisbon

My book splurge in Norway included Helen A. Guerber's *Tales of Norse Mythology*, which I'm enjoying immensely. Reminds me that some of the best myths began as stories for children. Example: *The Pied Piper of Hamelin*, which started as a tale about a magical piper who rid his village of rats. When he wasn't paid for his work, he turned his magic flute toward the children of the village, leading them all to their deaths. Moral: Don't neglect to "pay the piper," and be careful about following a colorful, charismatic person who might one day lead his followers over a cliff. We all know the story, but do we respect its timeless message?

Sunday February 24
Lisbon

Skipped church today, after last night's concert there. Did my river walk this morning and then settled into *Voyage of the Beagle*, which I ordered from Amazon. Never realized so many places in the world were visited on Darwin's big journey. Book starts in

Epilogue

Cape Verde, Africa, where I really want to go as soon as next winter if possible, and continues across the Atlantic to Brazil. Thick descriptions of natural wonders and enough travelogue to keep me interested.

Thursday February 29
Lisbon

Leap Day. Good opportunity to think about time and the fact that everyone's days are numbered. Peace lies in knowing who you are and being okay with where you are, what you've done and haven't done, and in all ways accepting yourself and the life you've been given. Praise God from whom all blessings flow.

Saturday March 2
Lisbon

Ten days before my birthday, I decided to rate my decades. High marks for the first and last ones; mediocre to bad marks for the interior ones. Does that mean it's better to be either young or old but not in between? Seems so.

Sunday March 3
Lisbon

Visited St. George's Anglican Church today for its 11:30 am Eucharist. Habitual and stoical but cognitively engaging. Marisa, who stayed at St. Andrews, doesn't like the cemetery one has to pass through to get into St. George's. I don't really have a problem with it. In fact, there is a kind of tenderness in seeing the resting places of so many people who wanted to be buried in the garden next to the church they loved. I read some of the gravestones while listening to chirping birds and rustling tree leaves. Met Marisa for lunch at a place we refer to simply as "The Ladies," who serve basic Portuguese fare that is always good. At night, received a call from my good friend Elizabeth, pianist at St. Andrews, asking why I've been missing so many services. Just a desire for some variety, I told her. It's more than that, but didn't want to get into it.

Monday March 4
Lisbon

Mondays have become our real "day of rest." We try to stay home, read, and have grilled fish for lunch. Rainy morning followed by wind and clear skies late.

Thursday March 7
Lisbon

Enormous horizon-to-horizon rainbow over the river this morning. Looked like some kind of heavenly arch welcoming those of us on the footpath but disappeared after about ten minutes, replaced by a strong wind from the west.

Friday March 8
Lisbon

Streamed the State of the Union speech from last night. One online newspaper described the president as "Biden on Fire" and "Joltin Joe." The Swedish prime minister was in the audience the same day Sweden officially joined NATO. Numerous dictator warnings about Putin and his puppets around the world. Still hard to believe the former American president said he'd let Putin "do whatever the hell he wants to do" against the European allies of the US. Historical statement, for sure.

Epilogue

Sunday March 10
Lisbon

St. George Anglican again for the morning Eucharist, and a stroll through the Jardin da Estrela across the street. Equal but different spiritually. Interiority feeds into exteriority and vice versa. Leave it at that.

Tuesday March 12
Lisbon

Today is my birthday. Seventy-one years ago in Detroit, USA, between 11pm and midnight on a Thursday, I was born, meaning that I dodged Friday the 13th by less than an hour. Josef Stalin died one week earlier. Musician James Taylor turned five that day, and writer Jack Kerouac entered year thirty-one. Happy childhood, normal adolescence in Florida, and a fairly routine existence thereafter. Became an expat to Canada in the 1970s, again to Scotland in 1999, and a permanent one to Portugal in 2016 where my permanent residency is up for renewal. Sometimes I miss life in America, mostly during the Fall months, especially the annual Thanksgiving holiday. But I wouldn't go back to live there. It's much easier to be contemplative here, which is mostly what motivates me. Moreover, with both the challenges and rewards of immigrant life, I never get bored or so grounded in familiarity that life becomes routine. I suppose my ultimate message as an immigrant bending in time toward the later years of my life on earth is this: I never, ever, ever feel old.

THE END

Lingering Question 12: How much is immigration about the journey to the destination, the destination itself, or the essence of what lies ultimately beyond the destination?

The Norwegian's Diary

Short Answer: Recalling Ollis Evenson's comment about *the New Jerusalem above* being his final hoped-for destination, it does seem reasonable to bring the subject of *eternalism* into one's ultimate sojourning thoughts. Listen to another Minnesotan, Bob Dylan, meditating on a hopeful destiny in *Beyond the Horizon*, a somewhat rare poetic glimpse into a future of welcome and warm embrace: *Beyond the horizon, in the springtime or fall, love waits forever, for one and for all.* I personally feel that way most of the time, adding that my wandering immigrant soul is preparation for something similar. Where this feeling comes from, I'm not sure. Perhaps it was always there. Perhaps it's the end result of a long-maintained faith, even a wavering one, nurtured by spiritual reading, hymn singing, nature walking, or simply by hearing others express hope about a future state of consciousness that follows the present one. I love its affirming guidance, and even some rather hard-boiled philosophers see eternalism as a positive way of thinking about eternity. I'm going to keep it, therefore, and allow it to be the main reason for smiling now and across time, even on rainy days.

From the Author

AFTER OLLIS EVENSON'S DESCENDANT, Christopher (who signed his letter "Chris," making it also possible the name was short for "Christian") wrote to me, I never heard from him again, though I would have welcomed further conversations about his ancestor's diary. Hence the personal, letter-like references to Christopher in the Prologue and Chapters Four, Six, and Ten. The years passed, and when I decided to revisit my original notes and transform the *Books & Culture* article into a book, I was unable to locate Chris, or anyone else from the Evenson family who may have been able to amplify Ollis's backstory. I would have had many questions about the diary, its missing years, the status of the original document, the location of dispersed descendants, and how the family understood particulars about their interesting, first-generation Norwegian-American. Without these desired supplements, a certain amount of guesswork had to be applied to the new manuscript, which I sincerely hope was reasonable, accurate, and true. The effort to shed further light on the subject matter was there. The question of how well I succeeded is admittadly a bit of an enduring mystery.

Selected Bibliography

Akhtar, Salman. *Immigration and Identity: Turmoil, Treatment, and Transformation.* Northvale, NJ: Jason Aronson, 1999.

Ahlstrom, Sydney E. *A Religious History of the American People.* New Haven: Yale University Press, 1972.

Altman, Ida, and James Horn, eds. *"To Make America": European Emigration in the Early Modern Period.* Berkeley: University of California Press, 1991.

Anderson, Charles H. *White Protestant Americans: From National Origins to Religious Group.* Englewood Cliffs, NJ: Prentice-Hall, 1971.

Anderson, Roger. *The Immigrant's Journey (Based on True Events).* Roger Anderson, undated.

Bangs, Nathan. *History of the Methodist Episcopal Church from its Origin in 1776, to the General Conference in 1840.* New York: Methodist Book Concern, 1840.

Bannister, Nonna with Denise George and Carolyn Tomlin. *The Secret Holocaust Diaries: The Untold Story of Nonna Bannister.* Carol Stream, IL: Tyndale, 2009.

Barton, H. Arnold, ed. *Letters from the Promised Land: Swedes in America, 1840–1914.* Minneapolis: University of Minnesota Press for the Swedish Pioneer Historical Society, 1975.

Beaken, Robert, ed. *Faithful Witness: The Confidential Diaries of Alan Don, Chaplain to The King, the Archbishop and the Speaker, 1931–1946.* London: Society for Promoting Christian Knowledge (SPCK), 2020.

Berger, Peter, Brigitte Berger, and Hansfried Kellner. *The Homeless Mind: Modernization and Consciousness.* New York: Random House, 1973.

Berry, Stephen R. *A Path in the Mighty Waters: Shipboard Life and Atlantic Crossings to the New World.* New Haven, CT: Yale University Press, 2015.

Berthoff, Rowland. *An Unsettled People: Social Order and Disorder in American History.* New York: Harper & Row, 1971.

Bittle, Scott, Jonathan Rochkind, Amber Ott, and Paul Gasbarra. *A Place to Call Home: What Immigrants Say Now about Life in America.* New York: Public Agenda, Carnegie Corporation of New York, 2009.

Selected Bibliography

Blegen, Theodore C., ed. *Land of Their Choice: The Immigrants Write Home*. St. Paul: University of Minnesota Press, 1955.

Bodnar, John. *The Transplanted: A History of Immigrants in Urban America*. Bloomington: Indiana University Press, 1985.

Boyer, Paul. *Urban Masses and Moral Order in America, 1820–1920*. Cambridge, MA: Harvard University Press, 1978.

Brown, Kevin. *Passage to the New World: The Emigrant Experience, 1807–1940*. Barnsley, UK: Seaforth, 2013.

Burrows, George Man. *Commentaries on the Causes, Forms, Symptoms, and Treatment, Moral and Medical, of Insanity*. London: Thomas and George Underwood, 1828.

Calhoun, Charles, ed. *The Gilded Age: Perspectives on the Origins of Modern America*. 2nd Ed. Lanham, MD: Rowman & Littlefield, 2007.

Choate, Mark. *Emigrant Nation: The Making of Italy Abroad*. Cambridge, MA: Harvard University Press, 2008.

Chrislock, Carl H. *The Progressive Era in Minnesota, 1899–1918*. Saint Paul: The Minnesota Historical Society, 1971.

Christianson, J. R. "Literary Traditions of Norwegian-American Women." *Makers of an American Immigrant Legacy*. Ed. Odd S. Lovoll. Northfield, MN: NAHA, 1979.

Christopher, Emma, Cassandra Pybus, and Marcus Rediker, eds. *Many Middle Passages: Forced Migration and the Making of the Modern World*. Berkeley: University of California Press, 2007.

Coan, Peter Morton. *Ellis Island Interviews: In Their Own Words*. New York: Facts on File, 1997.

Combe, Andrew. *Observations on Mental Derangement: Being an Application of the Principles of Phrenology to the Elucidation of the Causes, Symptoms, Nature, and Treatment of Insanity*. Boston: Marsh, Capen & Lyon, 1834.

Corporaal, Marguerite. *Relocated Memories: The Great Famine in Irish and Diaspora Fiction, 1846–1870*. Syracuse, NY: Syracuse University Press, 2017.

Cowan, Ruth Schwartz. *A Social History of American Technology*. New York: Oxford University Press, 1997.

Cross, Gary, and Rick Scostak. *Technology and American Society: A History*. Upper Saddle River, NJ: Prentice Hall, 1995.

Daniels, Roger. *Coming to America: A History of Immigration and Ethnicity in American Life*. 2nd ed. New York: HarperCollins, 2002.

Dary, David. *Red Blood & Black Ink: Journalism in the Old West*. New York: Alfred A. Knopf, 1998.

Dear, I.C.B., and Peter Kemp, eds. *The Oxford Companion to Ships and the Sea*. 2nd ed. Oxford: Oxford University Press, 2016.

Dreiser, Theodore. *Sister Carrie* (Third Norton Critical Edition). New York: WW Norton, 2006.

Emery, E., and H.L. Smith. *The Press and America*. Englewood Cliffs, NJ: Prentice-Hall, 1954.

Selected Bibliography

Fevold, Eugene L. "The Norwegian Immigrant and his Church." *Norwegian-American Studies*, vol. 23. Northfield, MN: NAHA, 1967.

Field, Iduna Bertel. *Rediscovered: A Century-Old Diary*. Decorah, IA: Anundsen Publishing Company, 2017.

Finke, Roger and Rodney Stark. *The Churching of America, 1776-1990: Winners and Losers in Our Religious Economy*. New Brunswick, NJ: Rutgers University Press, 1992.

Fisher, Shirley. *Homesickness, Cognition, and Health*. London: Psychology, 1989.

Gjerde, Jon. "The Effect of Community on Migration: Three Minnesota Townships, 1885-1905." *Journal of Historical Geography*, 5, no. 4, 1979.

Gjerde, Jon and Carlton C. Qualey. *Norwegians in Minnesota*. Saint Paul: Minnesota Historical Society, 2002.

Goodwin, Doris Kearns. *Team of Rivals: The Political Genius of Abraham Lincoln*. London: Penguin, 2009.

Gordon, Milton M. *Assimilation in American Life: The Role of Race, Religion, and National Origins*. New York: Oxford University Press, 1964.

Goffman, Erving. *Asylums: Essays on the Social Situation of Mental Patients and Other Inmates*. New York: Anchor, 1961.

Guerber, Helen A. *Tales of Norse Mythology*. New York: Sterling, 2006.

Hamlin, Christopher. *Cholera: The Biography*. Oxford: Oxford University Press, 2009.

Hansen, Carl G.O. *History of Sons of Norway: An American Fraternal Organization of Men and Women of Norwegian Birth or Extraction*. Minneapolis: Sons of Norway Supreme Lodge, 1944.

Hansen, Marcus Lee. *The Atlantic Migration, 1607-1860*. New York: Harper, 1961.

Hatch, Nathan. *The Democratization of American Christianity*. New Haven: Yale University Press, 1989.

Haynes, Stephen R. *Noah's Curse: The Biblical Justification of American Slavery*. Oxford: Oxford University Press, 2002.

Herman, Arthur. *The Viking Heart: How Scandinavians Conquered the World*. Boston and New York: Mariner (HarperCollins), 2021.

Higham, John. *Send These to Me: Jews and Other Immigrants in Urban America*. New York: Atheneum, 1977.

Hirota, Hidetaka. *Expelling the Poor: Atlantic Seaboard States and the Nineteenth-Century Origins of American Immigration Policy*. New York: Oxford University Press, 2017.

Hofstead, John Andrew. *American Educators of Norwegian Origin: A Biographical Dictionary*. Minneapolis: Augsburg, 1931.

Hutchinson, E. P. *Immigrants and their Children, 1850-1950*. New York: Russell & Russell, 1956.

Jasper, James M. *Restless Nation: Starting Over in America*. Chicago: University of Chicago Press, 2000.

Jones, Maldwyn Allen. *American Immigration*. Chicago: University of Chicago Press, 1960.

Selected Bibliography

Kantor, Mildred B., ed. *Mobility and Mental Health: Proceedings of the Fifth Annual Conference on Community Mental Health Research, Social Science Institute, Washington University, 1963*. Springfield, IL: Charles C. Thomas, 1965.

Kindelmann, Elizabeth. *The Flame of Love: The Spiritual Diary of Elizabeth Kindelmann*. Philadelphia: Archdiocese of Philadelphia, 2020.

Knaplund, Paul. *Moorings Old and New: Entries in an Immigrant's Log*. Madison, WI: University of Wisconsin Press, 1963.

Kobre, S. *The Development of American Journalism*. Dubuque, IA: Wm. C. Brown, 1972.

Kowalska, Helen. *Diary of Saint Maria Faustina Kowalska: Divine Mercy in My Soul*. Translated by Adam and Danuta Pasicki and George Pearce, George Kosicki, Gerald Farrell, Leo McCauley, and Francis Bagan. Stockbridge, MA: Marian, 2019.

Lagerquist, I. DeAne. *From Our Mother's Arms: A History of Women in the American Lutheran Church*. Minneapolis: Augsburg, 1987.

Lee, Alan J. *The Origins of the Popular Press, 1855–1914*. Totowa, NJ: Rowman & Littlefield, 1976.

Lindberg, Duane Rodell. *Men of the Cloth and the Social Cultural Fabric of the Norwegian Ethnic Community in North Dakota*. New York: Arno, 1980.

Loomis, Bill. "1900–1930: The Years of Driving Dangerously." *The Detroit News*, April 26, 2015.

Lovoll, Odd S. *The Promise of America: A History of the Norwegian-American People*. Oslo: Universitetsforlaget, 1984.

Mangalam, J. J. *Human Migration: A Guide to Migration Literature in English, 1955–1962*. Lexington, KY: University of Kentucky Press, 1968.

Marsden, George M. *Fundamentalism and American Culture: The Shaping of Twentieth-Century Evangelicalism*. New York: Oxford University Press, 1980.

Matt, Susan J. *Homesickness: An American History*. Oxford and New York: Oxford University Press, 2011.

Mauk, David C. *The Heart of the Heartland: Norwegian American Community in the Twin Cities*. Saint Paul: Minnesota Historical Society, 2022.

McMahon, Cian T. *The Coffin Ship: Life and Death at Sea During the Great Irish Famine*. New York: New York University Press, 2021.

Melville, Herman. *Journal Up the Straits*. New York: The Colophon, 1935.

Molland, Einar. *Church Life in Norway, 1800–1950*. Minneapolis: Augsburg, 1957.

Mullin, Robert Bruce and Russell E. Richey, eds. *Reimagining Denominationalism: Interpretive Essays*. New York and Oxford: Oxford University Press, 1994.

Munch, Helene, and Peter A. Munch. *The Strange American Way: Letters of Caja Munch from Wiota, Wisconsin, 1855–1859*. Carbondale, IL: Southern Illinois University Press, 1970.

Nelson, David T., trans. and ed. *The Diary of Elizabeth Coren, 1853–1855*. Northfield, MN: NAHA, 1955.

SELECTED BIBLIOGRAPHY

Nelson, E. Clifford. *The Rise of World Lutheranism: An American Perspective.* Philadelphia: Fortress, 1982.

Nelson, Lowry. *The Minnesota Community: Country and Town in Transition.* Minneapolis: University of Minnesota Press, 1960.

Newhaus, Richard John. *The Naked Public Square: Religion and Democracy in America.* Grand Rapids, MI: William B. Eerdmans, 1984.

Nichol, Todd W. *All These Lutherans: Three Paths Toward a New Lutheran Church.* Minneapolis: Augsburg, 1986.

Niebuhr, H.R. *The Social Sources of Denominationalism.* New York: Henry Holt, 1929.

Noll, Mark. *America's God: From Jonathan Edwards to Abraham Lincoln.* New York: Oxford University Press, 2005.

Norlie, Olaf Morgan. *History of the Norwegian People in America.* Minneapolis: Augsburg, 1925.

Norton, Peter D. *Fighting Traffic: The Dawn of the Motor Age in the American City.* Cambridge, MA: MIT Press, 2011.

Nouwen, Henri J.M. *The Genesee Diary: Report from a Trappist Monastery.* London: Darton, Longman and Todd, 2014.

Orsi, Robert A., ed. *Gods of the City: Religion and the American Urban Landscape.* Bloomington: Indiana University Press, 1999.

Osterhammel, Jurgen. *The Transformation of the World: A Global History of the Nineteenth Century.* Princeton: Princeton University Press, 2015.

Overland, Orm. *Immigrant Minds, American Identities: Making the United States Home, 1870-1930.* Urbana: University of Illinois Press, 2000.

Packard, Vance. *A Nation of Strangers.* New York: David McKay, 1972.

Park, Robert E. *The Immigrant Press and Its Control.* New York: Harper & Brothers, 1922.

Partanen, Anu. *The Nordic Theory of Everything: In Search of a Better Life.* London: Duckworth, 2018.

Perl-Rosenthal, Nathan. *Citizen Sailors: Becoming American in the Age of Revolution.* Cambridge, MA: Belknap, 2015.

Pickett, Kate, and Richard Wilkinson. *The Spirit Level: Why Greater Equality Makes Societies Stronger.* New York: Bloomsbury, 2010.

Preus, Diderikke Margarethe, and John Carl. *Linka's Diary: On Land and Sea, 1845-1864.* Minneapolis: Augsburg, 1952.

Reid, T.R. *The Healing of America: A Global Quest for Better, Cheaper, and Fairer Health Care.* New York: Penguin, 2010.

Reiersen, Johan Reinert. *Pathfinder for Norwegian Emigrants.* Trans. Frank G. Nelson. Northfield, MN: 1981.

Reynolds, David S. *Walt Whitman's America: A Cultural Biography.* New York: Vintage, 1995.

Ridpath, John Clark. *Ridpath's History of the World: Being an Account of the Principal Events in the Career of the Human Race from the Beginnings of Civilization to the Present Time.* Reprint. Creative Media Partners, LLC, 2022.

Selected Bibliography

Ritchie, Fiona, and Doug Orr. *Wayfaring Strangers: The Musical Voyage from Scotland and Ulster to Appalachia*. Chapel Hill: University of North Carolina Press, 2014.

Ritivoi, Andreea Deciu. *Yesterday's Self: Nostalgia and the Immigrant Identity*. Lanham, MD: Rowman & Littlefield, 2002.

Roberts, Sarah. *I Want to Go Home*. New York: Random House, Children's Television Network, 1985.

Rohne, J. Magnus. *Norwegian-American Lutheranism up to 1872*. New York: Macmillan, 1926.

Rolvaag, Ole Edvart. *Giants in the Earth: A Saga of the Prairie*. Reprint. New York: HarperCollins, 1991.

Roof, Wade Clark and William McKinney. *American Mainline Religion*. New Brunswick, NJ: Rutgers University Press, 1987.

Rosenberg, Charles E. *The Cholera Years: The United States in 1832, 1849, and 1866*. Chicago: University of Chicago Press, 1987.

Sandage, Scott A. *Born Losers: A History of Failure in America*. Cambridge, MA: Harvard University Press, 2005.

Sapolsky, Robert. *Determined: A Science of Life without Free Will*. New York: Penguin, 2023.

Scott, Franklin D. *The United States and Scandinavia*. Cambridge, MA: Harvard University Press, 1952.

Shukla, Nikesh, ed. *The Good Immigrant*. London: Unbound, 2016.

Skard, Sigmund. *The United States in Norwegian History*. Westport, CT: Greenwood, 1976.

Skardal, Dorothy Burton. *The Divided Heart: Scandinavian Immigrant Experiences Through Literary Sources*. Lincoln: University of Nebraska Press, 1974.

Smith, Anthony. *The Newspaper: An International History*. London: Thames and Hudson, 1979.

Stephenson, George M. "The Mind of the Scandinavian Immigrant." *Norwegian-American Studies and Records*, vol. 4, Northfield, MN, 1929.

Sundby-Hansen, ed. *Norwegian Immigrant Contributions to America's Making*. New York: International, 1921.

Szejnert, Malgorzata. *Ellis Island: A People's History*. Translated by Sean Gasper Bye. Melbourne and London: Scribe, 2009.

Taylor, Philip. *The Distant Magnet: European Emigration to the U.S.A*. London: Eyre and Spottiswoode, 1971.

Tebble, John. *The Compact History of the American Newspaper*. New York: Hawthorn, 1963.

Tocqueville, Alexis de. *Democracy in America*. Edited by J.P. Mayer. Translated by George Lawrence. New York: Harper & Row, 1966.

Vecoli, Rudolph J., and Suzanne M. Sinke, eds. *A Century of European Migrations, 1830–1930*. Urbana: University of Illinois Press, 1991.

Walls, Laura Dassow. *Henry David Thoreau: A Life*. Chicago: University of Chicago Press, 2018.

SELECTED BIBLIOGRAPHY

Wenzlhuemer, Roland. *Connecting the Nineteenth-Century World: The Telegraph and Globalization.* Cambridge: Cambridge University Press, 2015.

Whooley, Owen. *Knowledge in the Time of Cholera: The Struggle over American Medicine in the Nineteenth Century.* Chicago: University of Chicago Press, 2013.

Willis, Sam. *Shipwreck: A History of Disasters at Sea.* London: Quercus, 2009.

Wojtyla, Karol (Pope John Paul II). *In God's Hands: The Spiritual Diaries.* Translated by Joanna Rzepa. London: William Collins, 2018.

Wyman, Mark. *Round-Trip to America: The Immigrants Return to Europe, 1880–1930.* Ithaca and London: Cornell University Press, 1993.

Zempel, Solveig, ed. and trans. *In Their Own Words: Letters from Norwegian Immigrants.* Minneapolis: University of Minnesota Press, 1991.

Index

abolitionists, 79
acceptance, 30, 99, 105–6
Acta Diurna, 58
adaptability, 48
alcoholism, 49–52
America
   adapting to life in, 66–67
   American citizenship, 23–25, 31
   American determinism, 26–27
   Americanism, 48–49
   and Calvinism, 27–28, 32, 70
   civic rhythm, 76
   cultural progressiveness, 104–5
   ecclesial environment, 11, 33–41
   economic betterment offered by, 9–10
   emigrant drive to, 14–15
   external forces, 7–12
   faith communities, 10–11, 17, 33–41, 87
   faith opportunities and freedoms, 21–22
   forward-looking vision, 19–20
   and free will, 31–32, 93–94
   immigrant's hope in, 40, 82
   journalism and news consumption, 53–63
   labor experience in, 84–94
   mental health, 42–52
   moneyism, 12
   Nordic immigration to, 43–47
   political future, 82–83
   political movements, 16
   race and racism, 73–83
   remigrants/remigrant literature, 9–10, 22, 48–49, 91–92
   spiritual fulfillment, 10–11, 17
American Dream, 11–12
American Immigration Acts, 46
Ancestral Journeys (Manco), 68–69
Andersen, Paul, 37–38
Andersen, Roger, 3, 30–31
anxiety, 20–21, 43–45, 90, 92–93, 95, 103
Arminianism, 28
arrival-shock, 46–47
asylums, 48
attachment theory, 35–36

bad theology, 77–78
Bannister, Nonna, 4
binary philosophy in America, 59
book reading, 65–72
Books & Culture, 1–3, 38–39, 123
"boomerang" mentality, 48
Boston Gazette (newspaper), 58
Boston News-Letter (newspaper), 58

Cahan, Abraham, 9
Calvinism, 27–28, 32, 70

Index

capitalism, 9, 48, 63, 85, 89
churches, 33–41, 76, 87
civic crime, 74
Clausen, Claus, 37–38
The Coffin Ship (McMahon), 44–45
Cohen, Nathan, 47
Coleman, Richard, 75
Confucius, 101
congregational life. *See* faith communities
congregational life for Norwegian-Americans, 17
Cosby, William, 59
criminal behavior, 50
cultural progressiveness, 104–5
Curse of Ham, 78

Darwin, Charles, 52, 70
Decorah, IA, 28–29, 50
Decorah-Posten (newspaper), 56
Denominations and Denominationalism, 76
deportation, 47–48
destiny, 23–40
The Detroit News, 8
diaries, immigrant's
American citizenship, 23–25, 31
authenticity, 4
Calvinism, 27–28
commentary on American civilization, 7–12
disquietude, 95–101
ecclesia thoughts, 35–39
Elizabeth Koren, 29–30, 57
escaping vs. seeking, 17–19
Fragments of a Finder's Diary, 107–22
Iduna Bertel Field, 28–29, 65
illuminating history, 5–6
labor experiences, 85–88
long entries, 42
message-in-a-bottle diaries, 3–4

newspaper reading, 53–55, 57, 60
nostalgia, 13–14
politics, 16
race and racism, 74–76
religion, 21–22
remigration, 91–92
Roger Andersen, 30–31
short, repeating entries, 42
silence, 103–5
stand-alone entries, 42–43
The Diary of Elizabeth Koren, 1853–1855 (Nelson), 3
disquietude, 95–100
Divine Mercy in My Soul (Kowalska), 4
Douglass, Frederick, 60
Dreiser, Theodore, 5, 26
Drucker, Peter, 5–6
Durant, Will and Ariel, 70

ecclesia, 33–41
economic prosperity, 19, 66, 103–4
Eilsen, Elling, 37–38
Ellis Island – A People's History (Szejnert), 46–47
Emancipation Proclamation of 1862–3, 79
Emerson, Ralph Waldo, 27, 93
Emigranten (newspaper), 57
emotions, 31–32
Endo, Shusaku, 101–3
Epictetus, 101
escaping *vs.* seeking, 17–19
European expansion into the Asian world, 101–3
European literature, 44
Evenson, Charles (brother), 14–15, 44, 87, 90–91
Evenson, Florence (daughter), 96–97
Evenson, Halfdan (son), 96
Evenson, Hellen Andrea (wife), 96
Evenson, Henry (son), 96

INDEX

Evenson, Lillian (daughter), 96–97
Evenson, Ollis
  American citizenship, 23–25, 31
  anti-prejudice spirit, 60
  Books & Culture article, 1–2, 38–39
  and Calvinism, 27–28, 70–71
  disquietude, 95–100
  ecclesia thoughts, 35–36
  finding of diary, 2–3
  incident at Raymond and University Avenues, 7–12
  labor, 15–16, 84–93
  lay minister, 36–38, 87
  life motivation, 65
  and Lincoln, 79–80
  and Lutheranism, 38–40
  mental illness, 42–43, 50–51
  message-in-a-bottle diaries, 3–4
  motives for emigrating to America, 18–19
  newspaper reading, 16, 53–60
  nostalgia, 13–14
  parents' journey to America, 44–45
  public consciousness, 61
  race and racism, 73–83
  and reading, 64–72
  and religion, 21
  remigration, 91–92
  self-education, 66
  silence, 100–105
  spiritual frustration, 8–11
  and Whitman, 81–82
  work life, 64, 71, 85–87, 96
Evenson, Roy (son), 96–98, 100
Evenson, Sofia (mother), 96
Evenson, William Baldwin (son), 96
Evenson, William Bertrand (son), 96
expression-of- helplessness opinion, 105–6

external forces, 8, 28, 35, 70–71

faith communities, 10–11, 17, 33–41, 87
faith opportunities and freedoms, 21–22
family worship, 65–66
fear, 40
Field, Iduna Bertel, 3, 28–29, 50–52, 65, 101
Figg, Robert M. III, 25–26
First Amendment, 59
first-generation immigrants, 49
"Five Reasons Why You Should Read History More Than News" (Latumahina), 68
The Flame of Love (Kindelmann), 4
fluency, 90
Fragments of a Finder's Diary, 107–22
Franklin, Benjamin, 58–59
Franklin, James, 58
Franklin newspapers, 58–59
freedom, 48–49
freedom-of-choice decision making, 105–6
free will, 28–32, 93–94, 98, 105–6

The Genesee Diary (Nouwen), 4
Genesis 9, 78
Giants in the Earth (Rolvaag), 67
Gjerde, Jon, 31, 32, 89, 107
Great Depression, 103–4
Greeley, Horace, 60
grief, 98–100
Guerber, Helen A., 21, 118
Gutenberg, Johannes, 58

Harris, Charles Taylor, 18
Hauge, Hans Nielsen, 37
Haugeans, 37
Haugen, Einar, 103
Haynes, Stephen R., 78–79

Index

Hearst, William Randolph, 54, 60, 63
The Heart of the Heartland (Mauk), 88
Herman, Arthur, 77
history, 67–70, 73–74
home, 31
home construction, 88
homesickness, 10–11, 48
Homesickness: An American History (Matt), 9–11, 48
Homestead Act of 1862, 19, 80
honor and order, 78–80
hope, 40, 82
Hospital for the Insane, St. Peter, MN, 51

immigrants/immigration, 9–11
  destiny moments, 24
  ecclesial environment, 33–41
  Endo's Silence as an immigrant story, 102–3
  faith communities, 10–11, 17, 33–41, 87
  faith opportunities and freedoms, 21–22
  hope in America, 40, 82
  immigrants of conscience, 76, 79–80
  labor experience, 84–93
  lay ministers, 37–38
  literacy rate among Norwegian Americans, 15–16
  mental health, 42–52
  Nordic immigration to America, 43–47
  Nordicism, 76–77
  nostalgia, 10–11, 14, 18–19, 23–24, 35, 48–49
  personal letters, 5, 9–10, 22, 30, 57, 92
  race and racism, 73–83
  and reading, 55–57, 64–72
  remigrants/remigrant literature, 91–92

World War I, 100
The Immigrant's Journey (Andersen), 3
"The Imported Bridegroom" (Cahan), 9
incident at Raymond and University Avenues, 7–12
industrial capitalism, 89–91, 93–94
industrialization, 9
Industrial Revolution, 3, 11
insanity, 46–50
Irish emigrants, 15
Italian emigrants, 15

Japan, 101–3
Jefferson, Thomas, 59
Jewish immigrants, 9–11
journalism and news consumption, 53–62

Kearns Goodwin, Doris, 80–81
Kindelmann, Elizabeth, 4
Koren, Elizabeth, 29–30, 57

labor, 8–9, 15–16, 84–93
  and free will, 93–94
  immigrant labor in America, 86–94
  Lovoll on, 87, 91
  Ollis's work life, 64, 71, 85–87, 96
  reform, 88–89
  remigrants/remigration literature, 91–92
  and Whitman, 81–82, 84–85
  and Wyman, 89–91
land ownership, 19
Latumahina, Donald, 68
lay ministers, 37–38
Leaves of Grass (Whitman), 26, 81–82, 84–85
letters. *See* personal letters
Lincoln, Abraham, 79–83

136

Index

literacy rate among Norwegian-Americans, 15
loneliness, 46–51
Loomis, Bill, 8
Lovoll, Odd S., 15–17, 49–50, 56, 65, 77, 87, 91
Lutheran Church Missouri Synod, 76
Lutheranism, 38–39

Manco, Jean, 68–69
Maria Faustina Kowalska, 4
mass media, 62–63
Matt, Susan J., 9–11, 48
Mauk, David C., 88
McMahon, Cian T., 44–45
mental health, 42–52
Methodist-Episcopal church, 38–39
micro-marketing, 63
ministers, 56
Minneapolis, MN, 87
The Minneapolis Daily Star (newspaper), 57
The Minneapolis Tribune (newspaper), 57
Minnesota Inebriate Hospital, 51
The Minnesota Pioneer (newspaper), 57
moneyism, 12
morality space, 45

New England Courant (newspaper), 58
newsboys, 55–62
newspaper reading, 16, 53–62
New York Tribune (newspaper), 60
New York World (newspaper), 60
Noah's Curse (Haynes), 78–79
no-free-will opinion, 105–6
Nordicism, 76–77
The Nordic Theory of Everything (Partanen), 20–21, 43–44
The North Star (newspaper), 60
Norway, 13–15

Norwegian Americans. *See* immigrants/immigration
Norwegian Christians, 37
Norwegian Lutheranism, 37–40
Norwegians in Minnesota (Gjerde and Qualey), 31, 89, 107
nostalgia, 10–11, 14, 18–19, 23–24, 35, 48–49
Nouwen, Henri, 4

O Captain! My Captain! (Whitman), 81–82
old world traditions, 11

papistical insult, 37
Partanen, Anu, 20–21, 43–44
perseverance, 28
personal letters, 5, 9–10, 22, 30, 57, 92
Pillager, MN, 28
political movements, 16, 56
The Portugal News, 17–18
predestination, 31
press freedom, 58–59
The Promise of America (Lovoll), 15–17, 49–50
prostitution, 50
public consciousness, 57, 61
Publick Occurences, Both Foreign and Domestick, 58
Pulitzer, Joseph, 60, 63
Pythagorus, 101

Qualey, Carlton C., 31, 32, 89, 107

race and racism, 73–83
reading, 64–72
Recovered: A Century-Old Diary (Field), 3
Relation aller furnemmen und gedenckwurdigen historien, 58
religion and religious freedom, 21–22. *See also* churches; ecclesia; faith communities; lay ministers

Index

remigrants/remigrant literature, 9–10, 22, 48–49, 91–92
Ridpath, John Clark, 65–71, 73–74
Ridpath's History of the World (Ridpath), 69–70
right-reading mentality, 71–72
Rochester Hospital, 42–43, 51–52
Rolvaag, Ole, 67
Round-Trip to America (Wyman), 9, 48–49, 89

Saint Paul, MN, 2, 7, 13–14, 38, 74, 87, 90–91, 104–5
The Saint Paul Dispatch (newspaper), 57
sawmills, 88
Scandinavian-Americans, 50, 88
The Secret Holocaust Diaries (Bannister), 4
security, 32
silence, 100–105
Silence (Endo), 101–3
Sister Carrie (Dreiser), 26
slavery, 75–81
Smith, Timothy L., 11
Social Darwinism, 70–71, 73–74
social movements, 56
social-responsibility ethic of the American press, 63
Spanish-American War, 54, 60
spiritual frustration, 8–11
spiritual void, 22
stereoscopic technology, 18–19
Story of Civilization (Durant), 70
St. Peter, MN, 51
Strasbourg, 58
structuring, 78–79
subculture, 66–68
suicide, 48
Szejnert, Malgorzata, 46–48

Tacoma, WA, 14

Tales of Norse Mythology (Guerber), 21
Team of Rivals (Kearns Goodwin), 80–81
technology, 8, 18–19, 27, 104
temperance societies, 56
theodicy, 98–100
Theodicy: An Annotated Bibliography (Whitney), 99
Thoreau, Henry David, 27, 93–94, 101
Thrane, Marcus, 14
Thrane Movement, 14
Titanic, 54–55
travel exhaustion, 47
Trollope, Anthony, 5
truth, 4–6, 9, 11, 73
Twain, Mark, 26

United Norwegian Lutheran Church of America, 39
urban employment, 90–91
urbanization, 87
us *versus* them, 74–75

The Viking Heart (Herman), 77

white fright, 74
Whitman, Walt, 26, 81–82, 84–85
Whitney, Barry, 99
Winneshiek County Mental Health Association, 52
Wolfe, Thomas, 92
world history, 68–70
World War I, 92, 98–100
World War II, 103–4
Wyman, Mark, 9, 48, 89–91

yellow journalism, 60
You Can't Go Home Again (Wolfe), 92

Zenger, John Peter, 59

www.ingramcontent.com/pod-product-compliance
Lightning Source LLC
Chambersburg PA
CBHW070450090426
42735CB00012B/2505